THE OLYMPIC

The Story of Seattle's Landmark Hotel Since 1924

The Olympic
The Story of Seattle's Landmark Hotel Since 1924

By Alan J. Stein & the HistoryLink Staff

Photographs are reproduced with kind permission from
University of Washington Libraries Special Collections Division,
the Museum of History and Industry (MOHAI),
The Fairmont Olympic Hotel, and Paul Dorpat.

Special thanks to Neal O. Hines, C. David Hughbanks, *The Seattle Times*,
the *Seattle Post-Intelligencer,* and Alisa Martinez and
Beverly Magee of The Fairmont Olympic Hotel.

A HistoryLink Book
Design:
Marie McCaffrey, Crowley Associates, Inc.
Susan E. Kelly, Luminant Studio
Editors:
Priscilla Long
Walt Crowley
Jan Wright, The Wright Word Editorial Services
Supplemental research by Alyssa Burrows
Cover art by Heidi-Marie Blackwell

Print and color management by iocolor, Seattle Printed in China
First Printing, March 2005
Second Printing, September 2014
Produced by History Ink/HistoryLink
www.historylink.org

Contents

*T*he Olympic Hotel has been, and remains, a timeless symbol of the pride that Seattle takes in its history and in its contribution to the Pacific Northwest region. As the steward of this irreplaceable landmark, we believe that it falls to us to care not only for the building itself, but also for its longstanding reputation for service excellence and community partnership. Over its 130-year history, Fairmont Hotels and Resorts has demonstrated that it clearly understands the significance of iconic properties and is committed to preserving the integrity and prominence of historic hotels like The Olympic.

In recognition of the extraordinary history of The Olympic Hotel, we commissioned HistoryLink, led by one of the region's preeminent historians, the late Walt Crowley, to undertake the painstaking task of researching this hotel's incredible and engaging past. In working with author Alan J. Stein and HistoryLink's distinguished team of researchers, editors and designers, along with the collections of The University of Washington, the Museum of History and Industry, and others, we produced a book that is a fascinating and important tribute to this great hotel.

This book chronicles the 90-year legacy of the hotel and the significant role it has played in the history of the city and in the lives of its residents. The many important political and public events that have occurred in and around the hotel, and the unique relationship it shares with its landlord, the University of Washington, have helped cement The Olympic Hotel's enduring role as Seattle's civic and social center.

Of equal significance are the many personal and shared experiences of those who have celebrated life within the walls of this beloved landmark. Children have been introduced to the world, grown up, and marked the milestones of their lives here at The Olympic; a place that has been – and always will be – special to them. We are honored to be the venue Seattle chooses to celebrate life's brightest occasions.

The mission of great hotels is that of creating lasting memories. The story of The Olympic Hotel is not only about the brick and mortar where those memories were made, but also about the thousands of dedicated employees who, throughout the years, have worked tirelessly to exceed every guest's expectation. It is through their dedication and commitment to turning moments into memories that there are so many meaningful stories to be told.

So, as we celebrate the hotel's 90 year anniversary and continue our contribution to the story of this famous and beloved hotel, we do so with a clear sense of purpose and a commitment to the citizens of this great city that we will continue to care for and protect Seattle's most celebrated and treasured hotel.

Dennis Clark, *General Manager*
The Fairmont Olympic Hotel
Seattle, Washington

THE OLYMPIC HOTEL, SEATTLE, WASH.

THE OLYMPIC

The Story of Seattle's Landmark Hotel Since 1924

BY ALAN J. STEIN & THE HISTORYLINK STAFF

Chapter 1

ON DENNY'S KNOLL

ABOVE: *Territorial University, ca. 1870;* MIDDLE: *Arthur Denny;* BOTTOM: *Daniel Bagley*

*T*he city of Seattle got its start on November 13, 1851, when the schooner *Exact* dropped anchor off Alki Beach in present-day West Seattle. Aboard were Arthur Denny and a party of nine other adults and 12 children, the youngest of whom was six-weeks-old. Arthur's brother David greeted them. He had arrived two months earlier with John Low and Lee Terry to scout the area.

Low had returned to Portland with a note from David that read, "Come at once." During Low's absence, Terry went off to borrow a froe (an ax for cutting shingles) from nearby settlers on the Duwamish River, while David continued building a cabin. In Terry's absence, David accidentally cut himself with an ax, came down with a fever, and lost most of his food to skunks.

When the Denny Party arrived in the chill November rain, David — sick and bedraggled — was the only one there. The cabin was half-completed and had no roof. The women and children stepped on shore and the women sat down and wept at the sight of their new home. It was not an auspicious beginning for the founders of Seattle.

The first winter was tough for the pioneers, but they persevered with help from the Duwamish tribe, led by Chief Seattle. In the spring, most of the Denny Party relocated across Elliott Bay to what is now the Pioneer Square area. With them was David "Doc" Maynard, who had come up from Olympia at the insistence of Chief Seattle. Doc Maynard would become the city's first physician, merchant, postmaster, Indian agent, and justice of the peace.

In 1853, Arthur Denny, Doc Maynard, and Carson Boren (Denny's brother-in-law) filed the first plats for the Town of Seattle and established the present-day street grid for downtown Seattle. Maynard insisted that his property be oriented to the points of the compass, whereas Denny and Boren laid out their streets parallel to Elliott Bay. To this day, their mismatched roads tangle at Yesler Way.

Maynard's property took in most of what is now Pioneer Square. Boren's property lay north of Maynard's, and Denny's lay north of Boren's. One small section of Denny's claim would later become home to The Fairmont Olympic Hotel, but not before a university was founded there.

THE SCHOOL ON THE HILL

Arthur Denny was a leader in the creation of Washington Territory, established in 1853. Territorial Governor Isaac Stevens asked Denny's advice for the location of the Territorial capital. Denny recommended Seattle, but Stevens eventually chose the older, larger town of Olympia. In 1860, Denny worked on a bill with colleague Joseph Foster wherein Seattle would become home for the territorial university. The two men felt that this could be traded off in a year or two, and Seattle could get the territorial capital in return.

As they were finalizing their plan, Denny and Foster met Daniel Bagley, a Methodist minister who had just moved to Seattle with his family. Bagley convinced them that the university was a better prize. Later that year legislation was passed that would allow the university to be located in Seattle, "provided, a good and sufficient deed to ten acres of land . . . be first executed." In February 1861, Bagley was elected president of a board of commissioners whose job it was to find that land.

Bagley and his new friend Arthur Denny strolled through Denny's wooded property. A small knoll on the south end of Denny's land provided an excellent vista. Elliott Bay lay before them, and on a clear day, the Olympic Mountains rose in the distance. Denny offered to donate this knoll for the Territorial University.

The knoll was only slightly larger than eight acres, so the men negotiated to acquire two more acres from Charles Terry, Mary Terry, and Edward Lander, who now owned parts of Carson Boren's original claim. With 10 acres now in hand, Daniel Bagley enlisted the help of Seattle citizens to clear it of trees and brush, and then to erect buildings. The legislature would meet again in December; Bagley had less than a year to get the job done.

It took two months to clear the land. The cornerstone for the university was laid on May 21, 1861. Carpenter John Pike (eponym of Pike Street

Seattle waterfront with the university on a hill in the distance, ca. 1880.

and Pike Place Market) led the construction of the two-story building, as well as a president's house and a dormitory. The first classes were held on November 4. Bagley reported this tremendous progress as soon as the legislature was back in session. On December 31, a legislative delegation traveled to Seattle to dedicate the university, just one year after its approval.

CLASS ACTION

Hopes were high for the new university but the realities of running an educational institution in a rough-and-tumble pioneer town were difficult. Funding was a problem from the very start. The university closed briefly in 1866 for lack of money, and two years later consideration was given to leasing it out as a private school.

The university taught college preparatory subjects, comparable to a secondary school. It wasn't until 1876 that the first college degree was awarded — to a woman — Clara McCarty. That same year the school briefly closed again for lack of funds. Meanwhile the city grew up around the campus. Between 1860 and 1880, Seattle's population expanded from 302 to 3,553, but class sizes remained about the same.

Clara McCarty

The population grew tenfold again in the 1880s to more than 42,000 by the decade's end. On November 11, 1889, Washington became a state, and the new state legislature agreed that something must be done about the university. In 1891, they decided that a new campus was in order, away from downtown where the school could expand, as it should. In 1895, the University of Washington (UW), which now totals 639 acres, opened at its present site along Lake Washington.

WHAT TO DO?

University of Washington regents now had to figure out what to do with their downtown property. Seattle, like most cities across the country, fell into a deep recession following the Panic of 1893. Even after the economic boom brought on by the Klondike Gold Rush in 1897, the regents made no decision on how to handle their real-estate endowment. The land was situated only a few blocks from the bustling waterfront, but no one offered to purchase it.

In 1899, the regents decided to lease the property long term, rather than renting it out until a sale could be made. This decision survived three years of legal wrangling and internal struggles among the regents until, in 1902, they finally set forth a policy and formed the University Site Improvement Company to lease and develop the land for 30 years.

The University Tract was bounded on the north and south by University and Seneca streets respectively. Its west and east boundaries were the half-blocks below 4th Avenue and above 5th Avenue. The University Site Company's first construction project was the Seattle Post-Intelligencer (P-I) building on the southwest corner of 4th Avenue and Union Street. During construction, real-estate developer James A. Moore bought out the company's lease, and it was extended until 1954.

TOP: *Students and faculty on Territorial University steps, ca. 1888;*
ABOVE: *Territorial building columns at University of Washington, ca. 1914.*

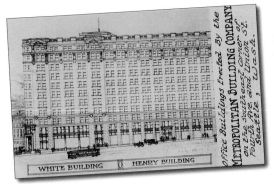

Although Moore had successfully developed many projects within the city — including the Moore Theatre, the Moore Hotel, the Alexandria Hotel, and the New Washington Hotel — by 1907, the P-I building remained the only new edifice standing within the entire tract. A new company called the Metropolitan Building Company was formed to take over the lease and to spur development. It did just that.

ONWARD AND UPWARD

The Metropolitan Building Company, under the leadership of J. F. "Jim" Douglas, lost no time in drawing up plans for the site. The first order of business was grading the contour of Denny's Knoll to prepare it for development. Office buildings went up. Work began on the White and Henry buildings, across 4th Avenue from the P-I building, and others soon followed.

Development of the Metropolitan Tract — as well as the rest of the city — received a boost in 1909, when the Alaska-Yukon-Pacific Exposition (A-Y-P) was held at the University of Washington. More than three million people attended the A-Y-P, and they saw a city with tremendous growth potential. Work continued apace at the original university property. The old university building was finally torn down in 1910.

Edmond Meany, one of the university's first graduates and later head of the history department, preserved the structure's four wooden columns, which were moved next to Denny Hall on the present UW campus. Meany and Dean Herbert Condon gave each column a name: Loyalty, Industry, Faith, and Efficiency, the acronym of which spells LIFE. The columns were later moved to the campus's Sylvan Theater, where they stand to this day.

Downtown, Douglas and his Metropolitan Building Company were busy transforming the old campus property into a commercial center, focusing primarily on stores and office space. The site where the old university building once stood was now empty. It took a few New York theater producers to shine a spotlight on it, and promote the possibilities of providing Seattle with a world-class theater.

THE STAGE IS SET

Vaudeville and theater had already found a welcome audience in Seattle thanks to promoters like John Considine and Alexander Pantages. In 1911, while traveling from Vancouver, B.C. to San Francisco, New York stage producer Marc Klaw stopped in town to visit an old friend. After being taken on a tour of the city, Klaw wired his associates Abe Erlanger and Charles Frohman in New York. Erlanger had financed early productions by both George M. Cohan and Flo Ziegfeld, and Frohman had made his fame by producing the first stage presentation of *Peter Pan*.

Klaw told them of his intent to build a theater in Seattle. The city already had fine establishments like the Moore and the Grand Opera House, but Klaw intended this new venue to outshine them all. The New York firm of Howells and Stokes was commissioned to design it. The architectural firm had just completed work on the Cobb building at University Street and

TOP LEFT: *Architectural rendering of the White Building and Henry Building, ca. 1909;*
TOP RIGHT: *Abe Erlanger, Marc Klaw, Charles Frohman;* ABOVE: *Metropolitan Theatre, 1912.*

4th Avenue, described as the first building west of the Mississippi designed exclusively to house offices for doctors and dentists.

Howells and Stokes based their plans for the Metropolitan Theatre on the Palace of Doges in Venice. The structure was built of brick, terra cotta, and marble. The entrance, with the marquee and a balcony beneath three tall windows, faced University Street. Inside, white Italian marble walls inlaid with mosaics and terrazzo panels lined the foyer. Farther in, seating was available for 1,650 people. A red velvet curtain fronted the 70-foot-wide stage.

THE CURTAIN RISES

On October 2, 1911, many of Seattle's finest attended opening night to see Edna Wallace Hopper and Richard Carle perform in *Jumping Jupiter*. The other star of the play was the theater itself. Prior to the opening act, Marc Klaw, J. F. Douglas, and UW regent John Higgins addressed the audience.

Higgins gave a history of the University Tract. Douglas told of the negotiations to build the theater and then introduced Mr. Klaw, who dazzled the audience with tales of life in the limelight, just as a stage producer should. He kept his audience rapt with attention and ended his talk by recognizing the other Seattle theater owners in attendance. Even they were impressed by the competition.

The next day, Seattle newspapers sang the praises of the city's new cultural center. The *Seattle Post-Intelligencer* noted that plans were in the works to build a grand hotel that would surround the theater. As it turned out, that dream took another decade to become a reality. Meanwhile, the Metropolitan Tract continued to prosper.

COLD AS ICE

Over the next five years, new buildings were constructed throughout the tract. Some were temporary and others were permanent. Notable structures included the Stuart Building (built for Carnation Milk mogul Elbridge A. Stuart) on the northeast corner of University Street and 4th Avenue and the Hippodrome (a display and meeting hall) one block east. In 1915, the Arena was built on the half-block north of 5th Avenue between University and Seneca streets.

The Arena was designed as a multipurpose structure, capable of holding large public meetings, convention displays, and — in the wintertime — ice hockey. A 75-ton refrigeration plant was installed to freeze pipes beneath the main floor, which in turn would freeze the ice on the rink. For a brief period, the building became home to the Seattle Metropolitans hockey team, which in 1917 had the rare distinction of becoming the first team outside of Canada to win the Stanley Cup.

The UW regents gave the Arena the cold shoulder, raising concerns even before it opened as to whether or not it was fireproof. They felt that the building should only be temporary until a more upscale building could be constructed to meet their expectations.

J. F. Douglas was proud of the Arena and fought for its permanency, but the regents rejected this idea. The building's lease would expire in 1925, at which time the regents planned to revisit the issue, in the hopes of tearing the structure down. As we shall see, the Arena would become part of the history of The Olympic Hotel.

ABOVE: *Cobb Building;*
BELOW: *Ice Arena.*

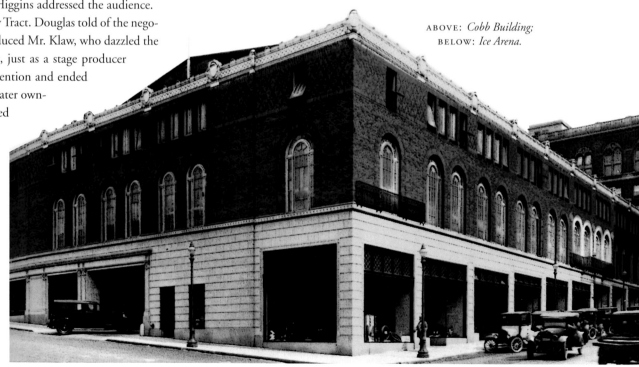

No Room at the Inn

At a time when Douglas considered the Metropolitan Tract to be halfway complete, World War I brought much of the ongoing construction to a halt. In 1917, Douglas told UW President Henry Suzzallo that it would take another 10 years to fill the property with permanent structures. When the war ended in 1918, Seattle — like many cities — suffered a short economic slump.

By 1920, the economic outlook had improved. The nation had fully entered the automobile age, leading to an upswing in the tourist industry. Cities from coast to coast were building new hotels to accommodate commercial travelers.

In 1921, Elbridge Stuart — now president of the Metropolitan Building Company — and J. F. Douglas wrote a letter to the UW regents proposing to build a grand hotel at a cost of more than $3 million. The building would wrap around the Metropolitan Theatre on three sides and would take up the entire city block. The proposal also recommended remodeling the Arena into a convention hall.

According to their plan, financing would be accomplished through the formation of a hotel company that would organize a bond drive so that anyone could take part by investing in the venture. The Metropolitan Building Company would bear half the cost. Local citizens would do their part to help Seattle prosper, and in the process, get a healthy return on their own investments. The company offered to waive any and all profit on the sublease, which made it a very profitable investment indeed.

Public response to the proposal was tremendous. The Seattle Chamber of Commerce immediately came on board and offered to help in

Elbridge Stuart   *J. F. Douglas*

any way, shape, or form. Local newspapers, *The Seattle Times* in particular, backed the idea 100 percent. Business leaders lined up too. And then — the UW regents turned it down.

To describe the citizenry of Seattle as stunned would be to put it mildly. The call went out to sack the board as soon as possible. Newspaper editorials decried the regents' decision, peppering their diatribes with such words as "ill-advised," "disloyal," and "blunder."

The problem with the proposal, as the regents saw it, was that it involved lease extensions. The leases for the Metropolitan Theatre and the Arena would be extended until 1954. Amendments to these agreements, they felt, would violate the public trust under which the land was endowed. Rentals were fixed upon the present lease, and any extension during which time the land became more valuable meant that the university would not receive money the regents felt was its due.

Once the regents made their case, it took time for Seattle to wade through the complexities of the issue. In the end, it all came down to one salient fact: Seattle needed a grand hotel. Concessions were made to allow the university to receive its due. Since then, the university has guarded this investment well, providing itself with urban real-estate revenues unrivaled by any educational institute in the country.

The university approved the amended proposal. The people of Seattle were ready to support what they felt would be one of the most significant civic improvements of their era. The city was about to receive one of the finest hotels in the nation.

ABOVE: *The Olympic Hotel, 1924;*
BELOW: *The Great Seattle Fire, 1889.*

$\mathscr{S}$eattle's first hotel was the Felker House, operated by Mary Ann Conklin, aka Mother Damnable. With a moniker like hers, it's no surprise that the hostelry did double duty as a brothel. Beginning in the 1850s, Mother Damnable's welcomed many a traveler in more ways than one. Beginning in the 1860s, other — more legitimate — inns were built.

They were built near the city's heart, and the Great Fire of 1889 destroyed many of them, including one of the city's finest — the Occidental, located at 1st Avenue and Yesler Way. It was rebuilt and later named the Seattle Hotel. It remained popular until the Pioneer Square area began its decline in the 1920s. The hotel was demolished in 1962 to make way for the notorious "sinking ship garage" opposite the Smith Tower. The loss energized local preservationists, who mounted successful campaigns to save the rest of Pioneer Square, Pike Place Market, and other historic landmarks including, much later, The Olympic Hotel itself.

As the city rebuilt after the Great Fire, new hotels were built, not the least of which was the Denny Hotel. Located atop Denny Hill north of Pine Street, the grand structure stood vacant and unfinished for a decade. Developer James Moore then took over the Victorian pile and renamed it the Washington Hotel. President Theodore Roosevelt signed in as its first guest on May 3, 1903, during a tour of Puget Sound.

Knowing that city engineer R. H. Thomson was determined to flatten Denny Hill to open up downtown Seattle's northward expansion, Moore hedged his bet on the Washington by building his more modern Moore Hotel on the hill's 2nd Avenue flank. He finally cut a deal with Thomson to permit the regrade of Denny Hill, but only after he opened the New Washington Hotel (now the Josephinum retirement home) at 2nd Avenue and Stewart Street in 1908.

Three years later, the New Washington was surpassed in size and quality by the Frye Hotel on Yesler Way in Pioneer Square. There was enough patronage for both, and most other hotels, as "the Queen City of the Northwest" boomed in the 1910s and early 1920s. The time was ripe for the city to offer new, more luxurious rooms fit for international celebrities, presidents, and royalty.

Money Management

On June 28, 1922, the Community Hotel Corporation was organized under the guidance of Frank Waterhouse, president of the Seattle Chamber of Commerce. The next day, full-page advertisements appeared in newspapers informing the community of the plan for public subscriptions. Gold bonds totaling $2.7 million would be made available, secured by the hotel's mortgage. Each investor would receive a $100 bond and one share of stock for every $100 invested.

Many of the region's top businessmen came onboard to help with the campaign. Among these men were aviation pioneer William Boeing, *Seattle Times* publisher Clarence B. Blethen, shipping magnate Joshua Green, Judge Thomas Burke, department store owner Donald E. Frederick, and lumberman Albert S. Kerry. Department store owner W. L. Rhodes chaired the citizens' committee.

TOP LEFT: *Albert S. Kerry;* TOP RIGHT: *Clarence Blethen;*
ABOVE: *Community Hotel Corporation note of appreciation.*

The subscription campaign was slated to begin on July 17, 1922. On July 3, campaign division leaders, team captains, and field workers assembled and listened to a speech given by Fred W. Graham, an agent for the Great Northern Railroad. Graham stressed Seattle's need for a noteworthy hotel, noting how the Davenport Hotel in Spokane raised the stature of that city. Although Seattle had many fine hotels, such as the Frye, the Moore, and the New Washington, Graham felt that the city needed, "a distinctive hotel to keep pace with the growth of the city and tourist travel."

"Seattle should be the objective point for all tourists in the Northwest," Graham insisted. "It should be the terminal and their outfitting point for numerous side trips. Seattle should have a great distinctive hotel and tourists should not regard Seattle as a way station on their route to cities with superior hotel accommodations."

Rallying the Troops

In readiness for the subscription campaign, half-page ads appeared almost daily in *The Seattle Times.* Some noted how all of the city's hotels were currently overcrowded. Others talked of investment opportunities. Almost all pointed out how essential the tourist trade was for civic growth.

Two days before the drive was to begin, 440 campaign workers — all men — met at the Masonic

Community Hotel Corporation correspondence.

Club in the Arcade Building. Each was given an assignment card with the names of prospects he was to call upon to sell bonds. Every Tuesday throughout the campaign, they would all meet for lunch at Koller's skating rink to tally results, which were then posted on a massive scoreboard.

The executive committee formally set the campaign to begin on Monday, July 17, though sales did not occur until Tuesday. Due to the committee's careful planning, the fundraising event coincided with an important anniversary in city history: July 17, 1922, was the silver (25th) anniversary of the Klondike Gold Rush.

SILVER AND GOLD

In 1897, the arrival of the steamer *Portland* carrying a "ton of gold" from the Klondike led to an unprecedented economic boom in Seattle. Twenty-five years later, the city was more than happy to recall the event, just as another boom was starting to swell. A huge parade held downtown included some of the "sourdoughs" who had trekked north years ago. A facsimile of the *Portland* sailed into Lake Union to launch one of the largest fireworks displays the city had ever seen.

The Arena was decked out like a Klondike dance hall. Inside, high-kicking girls cavorted and danced; wacky comedians mugged and did pratfalls. A Monte Carlo casino was available, for which scrip could be bought to play the games. The only thing missing from the Klondike days, thanks to Prohibition, were ample jugs of booze.

Spirits may not have been flowing, but community spirit was running high. On the first day, hotel boosters sold $1.6 million worth of bonds. The Silver Jubilee lasted for four days, during which time campaigners worked hard to raise the money. In just one week, they met their goal, raising $2,854,400 from 4,586 subscribers.

AND THE WINNER IS . . .

Despite the many people willing to kick in cash to support "the hotel," or "our hotel," by this time it was apparent that Seattle's new hotel needed a name. Wishing to leave this up to the people, the committee — with the help of *The Seattle Times* — held a contest with a prize of $50 to whoever submitted the best name chosen by the board of the Community Hotel Corporation.

The contest lasted all summer long, during which time 3,906 entries were submitted. The board considered all the names, including The Denny, The Gateway, and The Nisqually. But one name, submitted in several variations, pleased them the most. Multiple entries proposed The Olympic View, The Olympic Grand, The Olympic Arms, The Olympus, and The Olympian. The panel settled on The Olympic, for which 11 entries were submitted.

The first "Olympic" entry to be submitted was chosen as the winner. Robert Lee Ellzey, a local real-estate broker, submitted "The Olympic" on June 15th, the day the contest began. Informed of his prize by telephone,

Ellzey stated that he thought "The Olympic" was, "a splendid and distinctive name for a splendid and distinctive hotel." He then donated his $50 prize to the building campaign with a request that a portrait of Abraham Lincoln be placed in the lobby.

RAISING THE STAKES

In October, the new Olympic Hotel Company was organized, with a lease assigned to Frank A. Dudley, president of the United Hotels Company of America. Roy Carruthers, manager of the Palace Hotel in San Francisco and formerly of New York's Waldorf-Astoria, was hired as managing director, and William P. Taylor Jr. was hired as resident manager. George B. Post

ABOVE LEFT: *Gold Rush ship on Seattle waterfront, 1898;*
ABOVE: *The Olympic Hotel under construction, 1924.*

and Sons, of New York, handled design, assisted by the local firm of Bebb and Gould.

Construction bids came in at $3,900,000, well over the original proposal. Stock and bond holders were asked permission to issue more bonds, which they approved. On July 23, 1923, groundbreaking ceremonies were held at the northeast corner of 5th Avenue and Seneca Street. By the end of the year, the steel skeleton of the building was taking shape, and Albert S. Kerry was elected president of the Community Hotel Corporation, overseer of the Olympic Hotel Company.

Kerry had little time to get the job done. He wished to see the hotel completed by November 1, 1924, and he had to raise more money to do so. He accomplished the second task by convincing investors that Seattle would have an even better hotel than the one originally planned. He accomplished the first task by giving them that.

OUTSIDE APPEARANCES

Work progressed throughout the summer. The exterior was complete by the end of June. One portion of the east wing was left unfinished for further expansion. The building dominated the entire city block, rising 12 stories to the east, and 13 stories to the west. Even the glorious Metropolitan Theatre appeared small, now embraced on three sides by The Olympic.

The hotel was built in the style of the Italian Renaissance, but matched the character of other buildings in the Metropolitan Tract. The base was made of granite and black Belgian marble, with black and gold Italian marble above that to showcase the shops that ran along 4th Avenue and University Street. The building was constructed of buff-faced brick with a terra cotta trim.

There were two entrances. The 4th Avenue portal provided a view directly across the main lobby, and also provided a passage to the downstairs. The main entrance was off Seneca Street.

Seneca Street entrance, 1920s.

Marine Room, 1924.

ABOVE: *Standard guest room, 1924;* RIGHT: *Marine Room ashtray.*

INNER BEAUTY

The most notable feature upon entering from Seneca Street was the high ceiling of the great lobby. Walls were paneled in American oak. Flanking the entrance were two shops decorated in black and gold. One sold candy, the other, flowers. Next to the candy shop was the telegraph room, and next to the flower shop was the public telephone room with eight booths. Across from the entrance were the main desk, four elevators, and a combination newsstand and cigar store.

On the east end of the lobby a series of short steps led to the Palm Room. Beyond that was the main dining room — later named the Georgian Room. A towering colonnade embellished the entrance of this dining room and the interior was designed in the style of English Renaissance, accented by a blue and white color scheme.

Steps on the left and right of the main dining room led up to a balcony that ringed the lobby and a group of private dining rooms. The largest of these was the Junior Ballroom, paneled in soft, forest-like tans and browns. Other rooms had wallpapers depicting flowers and tropical birds, or they were decorated in American Colonial style.

At the west end of the lobby, near the 4th Avenue entrance, a grand elliptical staircase flanked by Corinthian columns of American oak led to the Assembly Lounge, which in turn led north to the grand ballroom, or Spanish Ballroom, so named for its Spanish style and design. The room was painted gold, set off by soft yellow lighting.

One floor below the Spanish Ballroom was the Italian Ballroom, which had the same dimensions except for a lower ceiling. Its dominant color was orange. A short flight of stairs proceeded down from the 4th Avenue entrance and led to the Marine Room, coffee room, and lunchroom.

BELOW DECKS

The Marine Room's columns, ceiling, and wainscoting were all made with weathered Douglas fir to give the setting a maritime flavor. Authentic ships' knees attached to the columns appeared to support the ceiling beams. Antique boat lanterns lighted the room, and a model of a medieval ship was suspended above the dance floor. Dining terraces were protected by railings designed to recall the rope guardrails found aboard sailing vessels.

Most striking, 15 murals adorning the walls depicted the maritime history of the Pacific Northwest. The paintings were the work of Edward Trumbull, best known for his 100-foot ceiling fresco in New York's Chrysler Building. The marine motif was also prominent in the crest of the hotel, which depicted a sailing ship similar to the *Discovery,* the ship from which Captain Vancouver surveyed Puget Sound in 1792.

Assembly Lounge (now Spanish Foyer), Lobby, and Spanish Ballroom, details, 1924.

Beyond the entrance to the Marine Room was the back entry to the coffee shop and lunchroom. Combined, these two rooms ran the entire length of the eastern side of the building. Both were decorated in hues of red, yellow, and grey. The main entrance to the lunchroom opened on University Street.

Across 5th Avenue, the Arena had been gutted and remodeled into a parking garage. Inside, a new system of ramps — patented as d'Humy Motoramps — was constructed, which allowed easy access via a series of staggered floors. As an added service, the Olympic Auto Store opened inside the garage to serve every motorist's needs. Another newfangled example of the burgeoning auto age was a tiny gas station built right in the middle of University Street, in front of the Metropolitan Theatre.

FINAL TOUCHES

The total cost of building The Olympic Hotel was $4,574,000 and it was built in record time. On November 1, 1924, Albert Kerry formally handed over the keys to resident manager Will Taylor in a ceremony that was broadcast nationwide on radio. Kerry then blew two long blasts from a Seattle Times whistle, and every light in the building was turned on for one hour to announce the completion of construction.

All that remained to be done was to install furnishings. Besides the public areas, hundreds of guest rooms needed accessories. The largest rooms had marble-front fireplaces. Fixtures varied from silver to crystal. Suites could be had,

as desired, with anywhere from four to seven rooms. Beds, carpeting, and bathroom fixtures were of the highest quality.

Appliances were placed in the hotel's five kitchens. Modern ice machines were installed that could produce the hotel's daily requirement of 40 tons, be it cubed, pulverized, or in chunks. Hidden from sight in the lower recesses of the building, the laundry room, storerooms, and other workspaces were fitted out with machinery, shelves, and other furniture and equipment required by those who ran the hotel. A maze of interconnecting passageways and service elevators allowed access to just about anywhere in the building.

OPENING NIGHT

Bondholders and stockowners got an advance viewing on December 5, before the grand opening the next night. For the gala event, reservations were issued for 2,045 guests, and sold for $10 each. The demand was so great that scalpers reportedly offered their tickets for anywhere from $50 to $100. Every guest room was reserved, some by out-of-town visitors, others by Seattle guests who just wanted to be the first to experience a night's stay in the new hotel.

On the night of December 6, lights placed on surrounding buildings illuminated the exterior walls of The Olympic. Two large spotlights on the hotel roof swept the sky. The Stars and Stripes fluttered on the rooftop flagpole above the white and blue house flag emblazoned with

Opening Night menu, December 6, 1924.

the Olympic crest. Inside, vases and jardinières filled with exotic flowers occupied nearly every corner and every table of every room.

By 7:00 p.m., the streets surrounding the building were crowded, both by those attending the gala affair and by others who just wanted to peek in through the windows and front door. For more than an hour, cars lined up to let off passengers. The men wore fine suits or tuxedos, and the women, elegant gowns and furs.

DINNER SPEAKERS

Dinner was scheduled to begin at 7:00, but once inside most people tarried in order to take in the lush surroundings. After checking their coats and wraps, they wandered about until eventually making their way to their assigned seats. Each of the four principal dining rooms was fully occupied, and since the eventual number of guests totaled more than 2,100, even the private dining rooms were pressed into service.

Speeches were made. In the Spanish Ballroom, University of Washington President Henry Suzzallo introduced Albert Kerry and Frank Dudley. In the Georgian Room, Judge George Donworth introduced C. D. Stimson and Gen. J. Leslie Kincaid, vice presidents of the Community Hotel Corporation and United Hotels Company, respectively. David Whitworth, president of the Chamber of Commerce, presided in the Italian Ballroom, and in the Marine Room, A. C. C. Gamer, president of the Washington State Hotel Men's Association, re-introduced Kerry and Dudley.

Dinner was served. Chinese maids in green silks moved from table to table. White-clad sailor lads bounded about, providing entertainment. Snappy bellhops in gold-buttoned uniforms catered to the needs of all, and a French girl vending cigars and cigarettes added to the cosmopolitan air.

Columns in the Assembly Lounge (now Spanish Foyer), 1920s.

Cutting a Rug

Four orchestras provided music. They were placed around the hotel so that each could be heard distinctly. William Hoffman, formerly of the San Francisco Symphony, was the hotel's new concertmaster; his orchestra was set up in the Palm Room. Max Fisher and his musicians played in the Spanish Ballroom, and Max Berliner's band played outside the Italian Ballroom. Down in the Marine Room, guests danced to Eddie Harkness and his orchestra.

Guests danced and partied throughout the evening. Once the night grew long, those savvy enough to reserve a room ahead of time had only to take the elevator "home." Others got into their cars and returned to their houses, sated from the experience.

Press reviews the next day showered the hotel with praise. One reporter for *The Seattle Times* stated, "Aladdin rubbed his magic lamp with a vengeance when he commanded the Genii of Community Enterprise to put before Seattle a hotel that would be the last word in comfort, luxury, and artistic beauty." Another waxed even more rhapsodic: "With the formal opening of The Olympic, Page One in a new social era was turned. Others may sing the civic anthem of praise and accomplishment; lift their voices or ply their pens in a paean over it as a monument along the endless road of progress a city travels, but there is also another point of view. In the province whence come social calendars, a capitol has been provided."

Daughters of the Pioneers of Washington. Also in attendance were several members of the university's first class in 1861, along with members of the Seattle Historical Society and the Washington State Pioneers Association.

Nearly 300 people assembled in the Spanish Ballroom. Professor Edmond Meany gave a talk on local history peppered with his own personal reminiscences. After lunch, everyone gathered outside the main entrance to the building, where a banner covered one of the pillars.

Following a dedication by Professor Meany, a young girl named Doris Lamping removed the banner, unveiling a bronze plaque, which reminded each visitor that the hotel was on the original site of the University of Washington. Years later, the plaque was moved to a new entrance on University Street, where it remains to this day.

Honoring the Past

One of the guests on Friday's opening night was historian Clarence Bagley, who, in 1861 at the age of 19, had helped his father Daniel clear the property to make way for the Territorial University. On Sunday, Bagley and his wife, Alice, were honored guests at a luncheon ceremony held at the hotel by the

ABOVE: *Curb service in front of The Olympic, 1920s;* LEFT: *Ad for Eddie Harkness in the Marine Room, 1924.*

Be Our Guest

From the very start, The Olympic Hotel was THE place to see and to be seen. Many of Seattle's high society could be found in the dining rooms, whether after a performance at the Met, or at a light lunch before a game of bridge. But most of all, The Olympic was a hotel that served out-of-town guests with style.

One of the first of many famous guests was Frederick Burr Opper, noted cartoonist of the era. Besides being the creator of *Happy Hooligan,* Opper was well-known for giving the world Alphonse and Gaston, whose routines "After you, Alphonse" and "No, you first, my dear Gaston!" delighted readers for years.

Opper arrived at the hotel on July 24, 1925, but the next day his visit was overshadowed by the largest visiting convention the city had ever seen up until that time. Not only would The Olympic test its mettle as the finest host in the city, the city would prove itself the finest host in the nation.

Storming the Castle

In the summer of 1925, the Knights Templar of the United States — a Christian fraternal organization connected with the Masons — held their 26th Triennial Conclave in Seattle. This was their 36th conclave since their first, held in New York in 1816. Thousands of Knights descended upon Seattle in numbers the city had never before seen. The Olympic was chosen as the grand commandery headquarters.

The city of Seattle bent over backward to welcome the Knights, who had been planning their visit for the past three years. A giant archway topped by a cross was constructed over 2nd Avenue at Marion Street, and a faux feudal castle was constructed in City Hall Park, south of the King County Courthouse, to handle registration. The streets were lined with 155 illuminated Passion crosses, with electricity provided at a reduced rate by Seattle City Light.

Atop the hotel, a giant electric Passion cross was erected. Constructed by the Knights at a cost of nearly $100,000, it stood 42 feet high by 18 feet wide. It glittered with more than 15,000 crystal glass jewels and a bank of blood-red Austrian rubies. Grand Master Leonidas P. Newby pressed a single switch in his room to light the cross, the street decorations, and a battery of 12 spotlights placed along First Hill. A giant cross also adorned the top of the Smith Tower.

OVER KNIGHT SENSATION

Nearly 600 high-ranked Knights attended a banquet in the Spanish Ballroom, while their wives dined in the Georgian Room. The Knights dined on Suckling Pig a la Crusader. Washington State Governor Roland Hartley, himself a Knight, introduced Newby, who stated, "This is the best conclave I ever attended, and I've been to fourteen."

The next day, massive crowds lined the streets downtown to witness one of the largest parades the city has ever seen. The Knights Templar marched up 1st Avenue, down 2nd, up 3rd, and down 4th to The Olympic, then back up 5th to Battery Street. Mayor Brown proclaimed the day a paid holiday for all city workers, but the state quickly informed him that such an act would be illegal. Employees wishing to see the parade had to use vacation time instead. Many did.

Throughout the week, more than 2,500 local car owners volunteered their autos and drove visitors all over the city. These cars covered nearly 60,000 miles over a six-day period.

The conclave was a major success for all involved. The Knights proclaimed Seattle as one of the most gracious host cities they ever had the pleasure of working with. In turn, Seattle felt good in the knowledge that 100,000 people from every state in the nation would be telling their friends about the fantastic city they had just visited. For The Olympic, this was a test as to how well it could accommodate a large convention. The hotel and its staff passed with flying colors.

THE HIGH AND THE MIGHTY

Over the years, many presidents have visited The Olympic. The first was Herbert Hoover, but only before he was elected to that office. In 1926, President Calvin Coolidge asked Hoover, then Secretary of Commerce, to visit the Columbia Basin in order to determine the feasibility of an irrigation project. Afterwards, Hoover traveled to Seattle to attend the annual meeting of the Columbia Basin Irrigation League, held at the hotel, before giving a speech at the stadium.

A commerce secretary may not have been the type to attract throngs of adoring fans to the hotel, but the following year a famous guest caused just such a sensation. On September 13, 1927, aviator Charles Lindbergh flew into town just four months after his heroic trans-Atlantic flight. Seattle — home to the Boeing Airplane Company — was one of 80 cities that Lindbergh visited to promote aviation and the building of airports.

More than 25,000 people filled the University of Washington stadium to hear Lindbergh speak. As they were waiting, the *Spirit of St. Louis* appeared out of the clouds and dipped low into the stadium, its wheels nearly touching the turf before flying off to land at nearby Sand Point. The crowd went nuts, and needless to say, didn't mind waiting until the nation's aviation hero returned by yacht.

ABOVE: *Knights Templar arch, downtown Seattle, 1925;* BELOW: *Seattle Mayor Bertha Landes and aviator Charles Lindbergh about to drive from Sand Point to The Olympic, September 13, 1927.*

Lindbergh spoke about the future of aviation and the critical need for Seattle and other cities to build modern airports, then traveled by car to The Olympic Hotel. Arriving downtown, the car paraded along 2nd Avenue as ticker tape and confetti floated down from all the windows. This was the first "paper salute" in the city's history. Once Lindbergh arrived at The Olympic, his first order of business was to buy a newspaper. "Well, boy, what's the news?" he asked the young news seller. Practically speechless, the paperboy stammered, "Oh nothing much, except Lindy's in town."

A crush of people wished to shake their hero's hand, and zealous fans tore buttons from his coat. Lindbergh quickly retired to the Presidential Suite atop the hotel and later invited reporters in for interviews. That evening a banquet was held in the Spanish Ballroom attended by 675 local business leaders as well as Mayor Bertha K. Landes. Upon the main table was a basket of Lindy dahlias, a new flower cultivated by the Seattle Dahlia Gardens in honor of his visit.

The next day, Lindbergh and the *Spirit of St. Louis* took off once again from Sand Point. He flew over Georgetown, where Boeing Field had been proposed (and was later built), and then over Renton, where he dropped leaflets. From there, he flew south, circled the capitol building in Olympia, and headed off for more speeches in Portland and beyond.

The Olympic Hotel brochure, 1920s.

BEHIND THE SCENES

Local newspapers often carried accounts of The Olympic's famous guests, but the job of staff and management was to provide service and comfort to everyone who stayed at the hotel. Very rarely did the public get to see how much work went into running a hotel the size and caliber of The Olympic.

On March 25, 1928, *The Seattle Times* did just that, with a full-page spread in the Sunday paper that mentioned some of the 500 people who worked in the hotel, and the tasks they performed to keep things running smoothly. The manager at the time was Frank W. Hull. His office had "as many speaking tubes, house telephones, and signal systems as in the conning tower of a submarine."

Mrs. Edith Gunby, the chatelaine of the hotel, headed a domestic staff of more than 50 maids from her office on the 12th floor. Each maid was trained to fold linens in the same manner and to place each piece of furniture just so. On each floor, huge chutes led to the basement, where the laundry room was located.

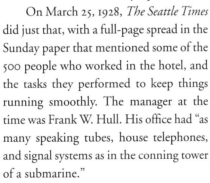

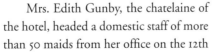

Frank W. Hull

WHERE THE MAGIC HAPPENS

Far below, in the sub-basement, chief engineer Joseph Davis monitored everything from temperatures in the rooms, to the efficiency of the elevators, to the quality of telephone connections, to the bulb replacement needs of every lamp in the building. Davis's men also ran a carpenter shop where woodworkers could repair cigarette burns to tabletops or fix chairs that may have been damaged by a "corpulent guest."

The aptly named M. Emil Burgermeister was the head chef, overseeing the dining rooms as well as the cafeteria and the employee's kitchen. Under his watchful eye were specialized chefs, such as the soup cook, the pastry cook, and the man whose job it was to make just ice cream.

Dishes were cleaned by steam bath, and after each use, silverware was placed into a burnisher, a spinning tub filled with shot that rubbed the metal to a high polish. In 1928, the hotel spent $400,000 a year on foodstuffs, and kept enough on hand to feed all guests for a week.

THE CANDIDATE

In the late summer of 1929, the northern portion of the eastern wing was completed at a cost of $500,000, and 300 new guest rooms were added, bring the total number of rooms to 756. Unfortunately, the stock market crashed a few months later and The Olympic — like many hotels nationwide — suffered for business. Still, people on the go always needed a place to stay, and that included politicians on the campaign trail.

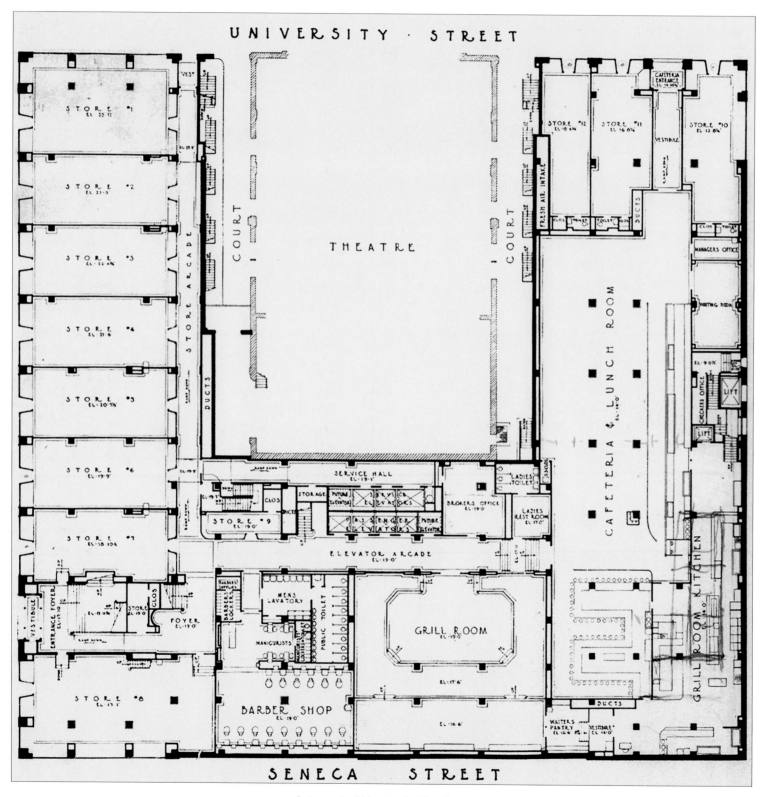

UNIVERSITY · STREET

STORE #1
STORE #2
STORE #3
STORE #4
STORE #5
STORE #6
STORE #7
STORE #8

STORE ARCADE
COURT

THEATRE

COURT

STORE #12
STORE #11
STORE #10
CAFETERIA ENTRANCE
VESTIBULE

CAFETERIA & LUNCH ROOM

FRESH AIR INTAKE

MANAGERS OFFICE

WRITING ROOM

LIFT

SERVICE HALL
LADIES TOILET
BROKERS OFFICE
LADIES REST ROOM
ELEVATOR ARCADE
STORAGE
SERVICE ELEVATORS
PASSENGER ELEVATORS
STORE #9

GRILL ROOM KITCHEN

VESTIBULE
ENTRANCE FOYER
STORE
FOYER

MENS LAVATORY
MANICURISTS
PUBLIC TOILET
BARBERS SUPPLIES

GRILL ROOM

BARBER SHOP

WAITERS PANTRY
VESTIBULE
DUCTS

SENECA STREET

4th Avenue-level blueprint for The Olympic.

On September 20, 1932, a train pulled into town bearing Governor Franklin Delano Roosevelt, the Democratic nominee for president. Roosevelt was driven to The Olympic as thousands cheered in the streets and threw confetti from the windows above. The crowd outside the hotel's main entrance was so large that the Governor was slipped in through the trades entrance on 5th Avenue. He rode a freight elevator down to the sub-basement where surprised soup cooks, busboys, and chambermaids looked on as he made his way to the service elevator that took him up to his suite.

That evening Roosevelt met with party leaders from the city and state. The next day he gave a speech at the Puyallup Fair and then returned to a packed house at Seattle's Civic Center, where he outlined his New Deal plan to provide relief and stimulate economic recovery.

THE SHOW MUST GO ON

In 1933, the Marine Room played a small part in one of the legendary tales of Seattle's theatrical history. On Christmas Eve, Katherine Cornell and her road company (which included a 17-year-old Orson Welles) was slated to appear at the Metropolitan Theatre for an 8:30 p.m. sold-out performance of *The Barretts of Wimpole Street*.

Unfortunately, her train, delayed by floods, didn't pull into Seattle until 11:20 that night. A few of the audience had long since left, but many decided to wander over to The Olympic for drinks in the Marine Room. As soon as the trucks bearing stage scenery arrived, Cornell's manager announced that the show would go on. Word was sent over to the hotel, and theatergoers returned to their seats.

The curtain rose at 1:00 in the morning, and the play lasted until 4:00 a.m., Christmas Day. Even though the cast was exhausted and hungry, they gave it their all. The audience was thrilled beyond description. It was a night to remember.

WINDOW SHOPPING

Aside from the Metropolitan Theatre, The Olympic Hotel shared its city block with several businesses. The October 1, 1934, edition of *The Town Crier* provided a glimpse of some of the shops and services in and around the hotel at that time.

South of the entrance was Littler's shop for men, which sold topcoats, suits, hats, and shoes for the finest of gentlemen. Around the corner on 4th Avenue, was Bacchus Luggage and the Pacific Coast China Company. The Olympic Hotel Pharmacy was located on the corner of 4th Avenue and University Street, and next to it was "Dr. Geo. R. Davis, Shoeologist and Chiropodist."

Other businesses were located inside the hotel, mainly on the mezzanine overlooking the lobby. Services there included a public stenographer, a photo studio, a beauty parlor, and a gift shop. Small businesses were also operated out of many of the guest rooms on the second floor.

A new addition was also visible atop the hotel. *Seattle Times* publisher Clarence B. Blethen had a "roof bungalow" built for his family at a cost of $103,899.08, which he then leased from the hotel. The Blethens lived there for only a few years.

GETTING BY

Unfortunately for The Olympic, most people weren't looking to buy top hats, luggage, or china services during a sour economy. The tourist trade was anemic, and by 1934 the hotel's finances hit rock-bottom. There they stayed for the next two years, until the 77-B Financial Reorganization Act worked its way out of Roosevelt's New Deal legislation.

The hotel came out of receivership, and instead of being a ward of the court, The Olympic became the property of the newly formed Olympic, Incorporated. By the end of 1936, earnings were high enough to pay two year's worth of interest on the first mortgage bonds.

ABOVE: *Presidential candidate Franklin D. Roosevelt arriving in Seattle by train, September 20, 1932;*
LEFT: *Katherine Cornell;*
RIGHT: *Clothing-store owner, A. A. Littler.*

*FBI Director J. Edgar Hoover (center) and associates
Clyde Tolson and Guy Hottel.*

Meanwhile, well-known visitors to Seattle continued to choose The Olympic Hotel. J. Edgar Hoover, in town on "hush-hush" business with the F.B.I., checked into the hotel on September 7, 1937, as did his associates Clyde Tolson and Guy Hottel. Some thought that they were here to investigate the notorious kidnapping and murder of Charles Mattson, a 10-year-old Tacoma boy. Hoover remained vague on the details of their visit.

ALL IN A DAY'S WORK

Since Hoover wasn't forthcoming with any juicy stories, the *Seattle Post-Intelligencer* decided to interview Olympic house detective Martin V. Collison instead for details on the kind of sleuthing that goes on at a major hotel. Though Collison had the highest respect for Hoover, he pointed out that even the nation's No. 1 G-Man might not be able to recognize on sight whether a couple was married or unmarried. According to the house detective, married persons spent very little time gazing into the depths of each other's eyes, and married men usually bought lots of magazines and newspapers before going up to the room.

Collison wasn't the only hotel employee who had to deal with the foibles and follies of each guest. In 1937, acclaimed Northwest artist Morris Graves — well-known for his outrageous pranks — performed a bit of Dadaist art in the Georgian Room. Graves entered the hotel with a baby carriage filled with rocks, to which he had attached a trailer of toothbrushes. Once inside the dining room, he placed a rock on each seat at his table and proceeded to order dinner. The other diners were quite confused.

In the early 1930s, a bellboy heard a hair-raising cry from one of the rooms. He grabbed an elevator boy and the two were creeping down the hallway when they heard the strange moan again. Fearing that a murder was in progress, they ran downstairs to the house dick, who gathered up the

hotel nurse and the floor manager. They hurried up, opened the door with a passkey, and slowly moved forward, expecting to be jumped at any second. They turned on the light and found a lonesome lion cub crying in one of the chairs. He missed his owner and traveling companion, famed aviator Roscoe Turner.

Guests who traveled with pets oftentimes led to much travail for the hotel staff. Once, a visitor from England entered the hotel with a shoulder-high Great Dane. Soon the dog was bounding about the lobby. Before he could be calmed down, he had smashed a chair, overturned a couch, and shattered three mirrors, six vases, and seven lamps. His owner was politely told to look for lodging elsewhere. Another time, in 1936, a pet skunk on the seventh floor caused all sorts of problems with the chambermaids.

THE PRESIDENTIAL TOURIST

In September 1937, President Roosevelt returned to Seattle, this time on vacation with his wife, Eleanor. They stayed in the Magnolia community of Lawtonwood with their daughter Anna and her husband, John Boettinger, publisher of the *Seattle Post-Intelligencer*. Meanwhile, The Olympic

Former President Herbert Hoover in The Olympic, June 1938.

Hotel became command central for the president's staff, and headquarters to the phalanx of press reporters that followed the president on his travels.

While visiting, the president did what many tourists do in Seattle. He and his family spent time at the Seattle Art Museum, the University of Washington campus, Green Lake, and the Ballard Locks. On a spur of the moment, the Commander in Chief even paid an unofficial visit to the soldiers at Fort Lawton.

Meanwhile, back at The Olympic, the president's staff was hard at work. Ensconced on the 11th floor, the president's secretary went through the daily mail, answered phone calls, and handled other presidential matters. For when Roosevelt needed to be contacted, a special phone wire was set up between the hotel and the Boettinger home in Magnolia.

Roosevelt took a side trip to Victoria, B. C., and to the Olympic Peninsula, but was never out of contact with his staff at the hotel. He kept in touch either by telephone or by telegraph. Morse telegraph instruments and teletype machines were also made available for the press.

RETURNING GUEST

The next year, another president made use of the hotel while on vacation. In June 1938, former President Herbert Hoover dropped in on his way to British Columbia for a fishing trip. He held a press conference in his 10th floor suite, and afterwards attended a special dinner given in his honor in the Spanish Ballroom.

Hoover spent much of the press conference criticizing Roosevelt's social programs, urging voters to elect "anti New-Dealers" in the upcoming congressional elections. Hoover also talked about his early work in the Columbia Basin Irrigation Project during his previous visit and he chatted about his upcoming trip north. "With things going the way they are," he said, "there are only two avenues to privacy left. They are prayer and fishing."

The dinner downstairs was restricted to state Republican committee members and heads of various Republican clubs. Former Governor Roland Hartley introduced Hoover.

VICTORY SQUARE

By the end of the 1930s, The Olympic Hotel was back on its feet financially. In 1939, the hotel made an operating profit, before interest and depreciation, of $185,622.10. Gross operating revenue was more than $1.3 million. Expenses, including rent and taxes, came in at $1.1 million.

In 1941, the nation went to war. On May 2, 1942, dedication ceremonies were held in Victory Square, which became a civic focal point for Seattle's World War II home front. Located on University Street, between 4th and 5th avenues in front of The Olympic Hotel, Victory Square replaced the old gas station, and became home to rallies, bond drives, and a war memorial.

A speaker's stand, in the shape of Thomas Jefferson's home, Monticello, was constructed at the west end of the block, and a 75-foot-high replica of the Washington Monument was built at the east end. Both were constructed through the efforts of local businessmen. The monument was inscribed with a growing list of King County war dead, continually updated as the war progressed.

ABOVE: *Some of The Olympic's original artwork that was sold in 1943;* FAR LEFT: Olympic Magazine; LEFT: *Ad for the Olympic Grill, 1940s.*

DON'T FORGET TO BUY BONDS

Throughout the war, Hollywood's most famous stars, going from city to city nationwide to stir up support for the war effort, stopped at Victory Square. Bob Hope spoke at Victory Square several times, as did Bing Crosby. Silver screen heartthrobs like Betty Grable and Lana Turner wooed the boys with offers of kisses to the men who bought the most bonds. The speaker's stage was also used for free concerts by well-known big bands.

Bob Hope first visited on October 1, 1941, and his stay at The Olympic was the first of many throughout his lifetime. During one of his stays, Hope commandeered the front desk and checked in several surprised hotel guests while tossing off snappy one-liners.

Another group of hotel visitors was the Quiz Kids, precocious young radio sensations who could answer just about any question. At a press conference at the hotel, Mayor William Devin introduced them and requested that each child in turn introduce his or her own mother and two members of the staff. "That's impossible," responded 10-year-old Ruthie Duskin. "If each of us introduced two, the last Quiz Kid will have only one person to introduce. There mathematically just aren't enough members of the personnel." Mayor Devin looked perplexed.

CHANGING TIMES

In June 1943, controlling interest in The Olympic Hotel passed to William Edris, vice president of the Skinner & Eddy Corporation. Edris — known by many as Carnation Bill due to his fondness for boutonnieres — had been a member of the junior board of the Metropolitan Building company when the hotel was built in 1924, and had been accumulating a stock base ever since. In 1943, he purchased the Metropolitan's block of stock consisting of 23 percent of the total.

Victory Square, September 1944. Victory Square was located on University Street between 4th and 5th avenues in front of The Olympic Hotel. It became home to rallies, bond drives, and a war memorial.

One of his first orders of business was to hold a benefit sale for Seattle's Children Home, at which he sold off much of the hotel's original oak furniture, bronze statuary, and porcelain vases. "What we need around here," said Edris, "is a little chintz."

The war ended in 1945. The Olympic Grill, which had stopped serving hot dishes because of a staff shortage, fired up the ovens again. Out in Victory Square, the speaker's stage came down, but the war monument stayed up until 1949, when it was demolished and hauled away. At the end of that year, Bob Hope made another visit, this time with his family and Air Force Secretary Stu Symington. After leaving the hotel, they traveled north to Alaska to entertain Air Force personnel on Christmas Day.

The year 1949 was also the year that Tubby Clark and Eddie Clifford first played at the Marine Room, which Edris had enlarged by removing a broadcast studio. "Clifford and Clark" opened on March 28, the first night that liquor became legal by the drink. Their piano and organ lounge act was an Olympic favorite for years. Back then, the Marine Room had a dress code. Men were allowed in only if they were wearing jackets and neckties. Problem was, a lot of men without ties were being turned away. General Manager Thomas A. Gildersleve solved the dilemma by asking his department heads to bring in all the ties that they had received as gifts, but never wore. Now any male guest could borrow a necktie, although it might be rather loud and gaudy.

Lana Turner thrills the crowd in Victory Square, June 15, 1942.

New Lease on Life

By 1950, discussions had already begun on the future of the Metropolitan Tract. The clock was ticking on the lease, which expired at the end of 1954, and the regents were bound by a law passed in 1923 stipulating that they could take no action without legislative approval. Working with elected representatives, the regents hammered out a plan that extended the lease on the tract for 35 years, effective November 1, 1954.

In the process, a new corporation was formed — University Properties, Incorporated — to manage the university's property, superseding the Metropolitan Building, Co. Meanwhile, William Edris had worked out his own lease arrangement with the regents, which extended the hotel lease for 22 years. In return, he would spend $1.2 million on improvements, including new elevators and the redecoration of the lobby, grill, and arcade. The penthouse would be converted to a suite of 21 rooms. In addition, a newfangled feature would be added to one-third of the guest rooms: television sets.

Sadly for theatergoers, improvements in the hotel signaled the final act of the Metropolitan Theatre. The 1911 structure no longer fit in with the forward-thinking plans for The Olympic Hotel and by 1952, it was already a moot point that the theater's days were numbered, and its swan song was on the way.

Chapter 3
A GOLDEN AGE

ABOVE: *Ice skaters perform in one of the banquet rooms, ca. 1945;* BELOW: *Georgian Room menu, 1940s.*

The city of Seattle celebrated its centennial in 1951, and General Douglas MacArthur was on hand to participate in the festivities. In actuality, the main reason for MacArthur's visit to Seattle was political. The general was testing the waters for a possible presidential campaign in 1952. Hotel staff would later claim that MacArthur demanded more protocol than any king or prince who had stayed at the hotel.

In 1953, the 45th annual Governor's Conference was held at the hotel, and President Dwight D. Eisenhower flew to Seattle to attend. Upon arriving at The Olympic Hotel, his first order of business was to go straight to the Presidential Suite for a family dinner with members of his clan. Ike had lots of relatives who lived in the state — mostly in Tacoma — and 22 of them had gathered for a feast prepared by Olympic chef Charles Eusebe. They dined on salmon, roast sirloin, Crab Legs Victoria, and Lobster Americaine.

After the sumptuous meal, Eisenhower excused himself and headed downstairs to the Governor's banquet. Guests and spectators were kept off the balcony overlooking the lobby so that the president could make his way to and from the Spanish Ballroom. The next day he sat in on the morning session, had lunch with the governors, and flew back to Washington, D.C.

FULL HOUSE

The week of June 6, 1954, was probably one of the most hectic weeks in the history of The Olympic Hotel, as well as in the history of Seattle. It began with the arrival in town of thousands of Rotarians from around the world for the annual convention of Rotary International. Their keynote speaker was Secretary of State John Foster Dulles. Although most of the convention was held at the Civic Auditorium, many guests stayed at The Olympic, where the organization held numerous session meetings.

As soon as the Rotarians left on June 11th, more than 10,000 Shriners swarmed into town for their annual convention. Known for their wacky hijinks, most of them came dressed as Arabs, wearing flowing robes, fake beards, and fezzes. Some rode on donkeys, others went around goosing the ladies with electric buzzers. A burlesque ambulance delivered a few men wrapped in bandages to the lobby of The Olympic Hotel, where the convention was held.

Topping it all off, The Olympic was busy preparing for a visit from Haile Selassie, Emperor of Ethiopia. Selassie had enacted his country's first constitution before his exile following Italy's invasion in 1935. When he returned to power in 1941, some considered him to be the Messiah. The Lion of Judah was checking into the hotel that afternoon.

EAST MEETS WEST

The Emperor arrived by plane in the morning, whereupon he was whisked to Boeing for a tour. From there, he traveled to the waterfront. While marching along the pier to inspect a military honor guard, a man in a red tasseled fez

walked by, waved, and yelled "Hi, Emp!" Selassie gazed quizzically at the Shriner and then turned to his interpreter who also gave the strange fellow a once-over. The interpreter could only shrug.

Selassie and his entourage — which included his son and daughter-in-law, Prince Sahle and Princess Sybel — made their way to a press conference at The Olympic Hotel, where the Shriners had already gotten down to business. As much as they loved fun, the organization's chief mission was supporting children's hospitals, seeking new ways to raise money and give hope to the children who needed it most. Selassie got briefed on Shriner history and Shriner behavior and later explained through his interpreter that he liked the colorful dress of the men, as well as their enthusiasm.

The next day, the Emperor rested in his room and took care of correspondence, while the Prince and Princess explored the city and went shopping. At the same time, the Shriners were up to their old tricks. Some of them popped open a manhole cover at 4th Avenue and Pike Street, and dipped fishing poles into the sewer. Nearby, another group placed a table in the middle of Pike Street and took their tea while traffic whizzed by. Back at the hotel, one of the men amused himself with a little device that slipped easily into an unsuspecting bystander's pocket. It was a siren that got louder and louder for a full minute, and could not be turned off.

A good time was had by all. The Shriners enjoyed their stay, as did the Emperor, who tipped the staff with gold coins. The Olympic was a hotel that could be enjoyed by revelers and royalty alike.

THE CURTAIN FALLS

On November 1, 1954, the new 35-year lease on the Metropolitan Tract went into effect, as did William Edris's 22-year lease on The Olympic. Edris had already begun improving the hotel and was looking to sell his interest. Fortunately for him, Western Hotels — the operators of Seattle's Mayflower, Benjamin Franklin, Roosevelt, and New Washington hotels — was looking to buy. On August 1, 1955, the sale of the hotel was approved.

TOP: *General Douglas MacArthur visits the hotel, 1951;* LEFT: *Emperor Haile Selassie broadcasts over KOMO from one of the meeting rooms, 1954;* ABOVE: *Metropolitan Theatre during demolition, 1956.*

Eddie Carlson, president of Western Hotels, submitted a new plan for improvements. The Metropolitan Theatre would be torn down to make way for a drive-in entrance on University Street. Above the entrance, a new ballroom would be built, twice the size of the Spanish Ballroom. A formal garden would be installed on the roof of the new addition. On the corner of 5th Avenue and University Street, a new restaurant called the Golden Lion would replace the Olympic Grill. Finally, the Italian Ballroom would be remodeled into the Olympic Bowl.

On December 4, 1954, the curtain came down on the Metropolitan Theatre, with a performance by Helen Hayes in *What Every Woman Knows.* For more than a year before demolition began, the grand building that had once held performances by Al Jolson, Geraldine Farrar, Boris Karloff, and Ethel Barrymore stood empty.

THEY LIKE IKE

In the fall of 1956, President Eisenhower made another visit to The Olympic, this time on the campaign trail. His wife, Mamie, accompanied him. Hotel management spent almost a month preparing for their visit. The executive suite received a fresh coat of lime-green paint and new furnishings, and a special telephone was installed that provided a hot line directly to the White House.

TOP: *A fresh batch of hard rolls from The Olympic's ovens, ca. 1960;*
ABOVE: *Society women dining in the Georgian Room, 1948.*

The Secret Service screened all of the hotel's 625 employees. Rooms were set aside for the president's valet, press secretary, and physician, among others. Bellhops carried more than 200 pieces of luggage belonging to the president's staff and the press. In all, 23 rooms were reserved on the 11th floor. One room was converted into a parlor for Mrs. Eisenhower, with new cherry-wood furniture and white silk shades.

Chef Charles Eusebe and his kitchen staff were kept busy throughout the stay. On the first night, Ike and Mamie dined on Chicken a la King and crab legs. Mrs. Eisenhower noted that she especially enjoyed the hard rolls, which were exclusively baked for the hotel.

At the Civic Auditorium (now Marion McCaw Hall), President Eisenhower gave one of the hardest-hitting speeches of the campaign year. He never once mentioned the name of his opponent, Adlai Stevenson, but made light of many of Stevenson's promises. Back at The Olympic Hotel, the Junior Ballroom filled with the clatter of typewriters and teletype machines as reporters sent details of his speech around the nation.

GRAND OPENING

On August 1, 1957, the Grand Ballroom was formally opened with a benefit for the Ryther Four and Twenty Club, which raised funds for the Ryther Child Center. Over the years, The Olympic Hotel has held many benefits related to children's health care, most notably Children's Orthopedic Hospital, which always held its most gala fundraisers there.

Guests at the Ryther Ball enjoyed a fashion show that featured the furs, fabrics, and frills of the future. Four "jewel girls" opened the show wearing more than a million dollars worth of diamonds, emeralds, pearls, and rubies. Some of the biggest fashion names in the country designed the dresses models wore in the cavalcade of color.

But the star of the evening was the massive Grand Ballroom itself, located above the soon-to-be-opened University Street entrance. Tables were festooned with carnation bouquets and miniature buildings of Seattle's "futurama" designed by art students in public schools. Attendees also got their first glimpse of the modern art murals on the south wall, which were designed and executed by Northwest artist Jean Beall, assisted by Doris Chase.

ONE IN EVERY CROWD

On August 20, 1957, dedication ceremonies were held at The Olympic's new University Street entrance. More than a thousand people filled University Plaza as Jackie Souders' Olympic Band played "Bow Down to Washington," the university fight song. Speeches were delivered by Lieutenant Governor

Grand opening of the University Street entrance, August 27, 1957.

Jean Beall discusses her mural in the Grand Ballroom with managing director Thomas A. Gildersleve, 1957.

John Cherburg, Seattle City Council President David Levine, Seattle Chamber of Commerce President Joseph Gandy, and University of Washington President Dr. Henry Schmitz.

Just as Western Hotels President S. W. Thurston finished the last speech, an explosion went off atop the hotel, spraying thousands of bits of confetti onto the crowd below. The speakers entered three cars and drove into the new entrance, christening it.

As paper rained down, the crowd cheered, all except for one curmudgeon in the audience. Interviewed by a reporter from the *Seattle Post-Intelligencer,* the old-timer grumbled that Katherine Cornell would never stand for this. He recalled her legendary Christmas morn performance in 1933.

THE CENTER OF ATTENTION

Who else should return in 1958 but perennial guest, Bob Hope? The Seattle-loving comedian was chosen as that year's Grand Marshal for the Seafair Parade, although at the King's Dinner held in the new Grand Ballroom, Hope jokingly pretended that he came to Seafair under protest. "At home, every time I picked up a telephone, there was [Seafair chairman] Bob Littler on the wire. I had to go through him to get an outside line."

Of course, not all meetings at the hotel were fun and games. Two months later, The Olympic hosted the Colombo Plan's annual advisory meeting. Created in 1951, the organization focused on strengthening the social and economic development of the nations of Southeast Asia and the Pacific. Flags of all 21 participating countries were displayed in the hotel, where delegates met and discussed their plans with Secretary of State John Foster Dulles. The organization presaged America's deepening involvement in Southeast Asia.

Also in 1958, two Olympic Grill patrons were given recognition for their loyalty. At a hotel ceremony that commemorated the long service of many of its employees, it was pointed out that the two gentlemen had eaten lunch at the grill almost every day for 30 years. Albert Koepfli and A. C. Devoe, partners in Seattle Plumbing Supply, were formally dubbed Knights of The Olympic, a high honor indeed.

THE PRINCE AND PRINCESS

The year 1960 saw another presidential campaign, along with visits to the hotel by both Richard Nixon and John F. Kennedy. But neither the vice president nor the senator from Massachusetts could compare to Crown Prince Akihito and Crown Princess Michiko of Japan, who toured the United States to commemorate the centennial of the first trade and friendship treaty between the two countries. Their Imperial Highnesses arrived in Seattle on October 4, 1960, and thousands turned out to witness a rare visit by Japanese royalty.

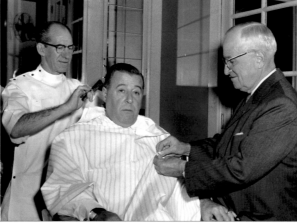

Governor Albert Rosellini greeted the royal couple at the airport, and from there they were driven to The Olympic Hotel. A red carpet was laid on University Street for their arrival at University Plaza. A 45-minute welcoming ceremony was held, during which time Akihito and Michiko sat in gold-colored thrones decorated with dolphins. Among the speakers were Senator Warren Magnuson and Representative Thomas Pelly.

That evening, 837 guests attended a royal banquet in the Grand Ballroom. The head table alone had seats for 47 persons of honor. All tables were covered with pink cloths, offset by vases filled with red carnations. Attendees dined on roast filet mignon. Prince Akihito stated that he and his wife were very happy that Seattle was included in their itinerary.

A Day with the Royals

The next morning, maitre d'hotel Norman Lavin was surprised when the Imperial couple ordered hotcakes and waffles for breakfast, but then realized that this was like Americans visiting Italy and ordering pasta. Before the day's planned events, Prince Akihito made an unscheduled shopping trip to Frederick & Nelson, where he bought some books.

After checking out of the hotel, the couple traveled to the tea garden at the University of Washington Arboretum. There, in a formal ceremony, they planted a cherry tree and a white birch. The Princess left to visit the Seattle Art Museum in Volunteer Park, while the Prince boarded a Coast Guard patrol boat at the foot of Madison Street, which took him across Lake Washington to the Boeing plant in Renton.

Everywhere they went, heads turned to catch a glimpse of the handsome prince and his lovely bride. Only as they flew out of Sea-Tac Airport did they break protocol, waving energetically from the airplane window, obviously pleased with their stay. Nearly 30 years later, Prince Akihito became Emperor of Japan following the death of his father Hirohito in 1989.

Harry about Town

A few weeks after the royal visit, former President Truman stayed at the hotel while campaigning for John F. Kennedy. After a restful night in the Presidential Suite, the 76-year-old statesman awoke early in the morning for his morning constitutional — a brisk walk around downtown Seattle.

Leaving the hotel, Truman walked north along 5th Avenue to Pike Street, west to 4th Avenue, and down 4th Avenue to Spring Street before returning to the hotel. Surprised passersby greeted Mr. Truman, and many shook his hand. Truman noted that, "People are nice. I don't want anything and don't have anything to give away, but they're nice and I appreciate it."

Back at The Olympic Hotel, Truman had a breakfast meeting with more than 50 of the state's top labor leaders. He let them know that before he left Missouri, his wife had warned him to clean up his language. Recently, while visiting in Texas, he'd told voters that if they did not vote for Kennedy, "they could go to hell." On this trip Truman made sure to tone it down a notch. Afterwards, he got a haircut at The Olympic's barbershop while chatting with Senator Warren Magnuson.

Jack Be Nimble

John F. Kennedy won the election and in November 1961, made his only visit to Seattle while in office to help celebrate the centennial of the University of Washington's founding on the site of The Olympic Hotel. Tens of thousands lined the streets as the presidential cavalcade rolled through downtown. The largest crowd was in University Plaza, where Kennedy and his staff briefly stopped to arrange their suite into what they officially called the "Seattle White House." The Olympic staff had to make a special rush order to Tacoma for a copy of the president's favorite rocking chair and a special mattress for his back troubles.

President Kennedy then proceeded to the University of Washington's Hec Edmundsen Pavilion where he gave a major foreign policy speech at the University of Washington Centennial Convocation — his first talk in the Western United States since his inauguration. The president spoke firmly about relations with the Soviet Union, and the challenges that lay ahead.

After the speech the president returned to The Olympic Hotel where he spoke at a dinner honoring Senator Warren Magnuson's 25th Anniversary of Congressional service. Nearly 3,000 people paid $100 for dinner: The Olympic Hotel could not seat them all. Every ballroom and six smaller dining rooms were filled and additional tables were set up on the Hotel's mezzanine. The overflow went to Victor Rosellini's 410 Restaurant across the street. Most of the diners saw the talk on closed circuit television. President Kennedy stated, "No man has done more to transform the face of this state in the last 25 years than your senior senator."

SEE YOU AT THE FAIR

Throughout 1961, most people were preoccupied with construction going on just north of downtown, especially the Space Needle towering above it all. Businesses throughout the city started getting ready for the millions of visitors expected for the upcoming World's Fair. As part of the city's beautification campaign, The Olympic Hotel was the first building to have its exterior scrubbed and polished. The Seattle World's Fair — known as Century 21 — opened on April 21, 1962.

The hotel was ready, thanks in no small part to the fact that Eddie Carlson was also president of the World's Fair Commission during its planning stages. In fact, most of the World's Fair was planned in the Seattle Room behind the Olympic Grill, which became the impetus for Civic Seattle's 7:30 breakfast meetings for years to come. Throughout the summer of 1962, many of the fair's most famous visitors stayed at The Olympic Hotel.

The Golden Lion opened for business, highlighted by the musical stylings of Marine Room favorites Eddie and Tubby. Eddie Clifford died one year later, but Tubby Clark played on for many more years. The Golden Lion was a favorite for those with a discerning palette. Besides the 85 entries on the wine list, the restaurant served many unique dishes, including barbecued salmon sandwiches covered in melted cheese, and Golden Lion Soup, made

Eddie Carlson (seated far right next to Warren Magnuson) looks over a 1962 World's Fair poster. J. F. Douglas (seated far left) looks on.

New seafood bar in the Marine Room, 1962.

with oysters, clam nectar, and whipped cream. In 1961, the dining establishment made headlines when a woman who helped organize Seattle's Women's Amateur Athletic League visited it. Her name was Golden Lyon.

Meanwhile, the Marine Room was completely remodeled. Gone was the horseshoe bar; in its place was a stage for top-notch performers. Drinks were served at a bar along the side wall, and a seafood bar was added. Opening acts on the first night were the Gloria Tracy Combo, comedy musicians Somethin' Smith and the Redheads, and the Windsor Duo, with Mickey Turner on accordion accompanied by Bonnie Vale on the cocktail drums.

CLOCKWISE FROM TOP LEFT: *At an Olympic banquet, President John F. Kennedy celebrates Senator Warren Magnuson's 25th year in Congress, November 16, 1961; Governor Nelson Rockefeller at The Olympic, May 10, 1962; Barry Goldwater meets with youthful supporters outside his suite, September 9, 1964; John Glenn takes a ride on the monorail, May 10, 1962.*

ROCKET MAN

Only a few weeks after the fair opened, The Olympic Hotel was bursting with celebrities. On May 9, New York Governor Nelson Rockefeller checked in for the next day's New York State Day at the fair. Vice President Lyndon Johnson was already in his suite, but was nursing a sore throat he developed while dedicating Ice Harbor Dam near Pasco. Other rooms were assigned to numerous NASA officials, including rocket scientist Dr. Werner von Braun, and some of the test pilots involved in the space program.

The next morning, astronaut John Glenn showed up, having spent the night at the house of an old flying buddy. Over a thousand people were gathered outside the hotel to catch a glimpse of the first American to orbit the globe — a feat that he'd accomplished less than three months earlier. After meeting with Governor Rosellini and Senator Magnuson at the hotel, Glenn traveled with them to the fair by monorail.

Glenn saw the sights and participated in a NASA panel discussion at the Opera House, and then returned to The Olympic Hotel for a special NASA dinner in the Grand Ballroom attended by 800 guests. Comedian Bill Dana was one of the speakers, and had everyone laughing with his astronaut character, Jose Jimenez, from the *Steve Allen Show*.

The audience heard talks from scientists, politicians, and pilots, as well as from John Glenn. Earlier in the day, when Glenn was seated next to the eight test pilots, the *Seattle Post-Intelligencer* noted that, "they might as well have been eight guys named Joe." Unknown to the audience at the time, one of those anonymous Joes was none other than Neil Armstrong, who on July 20, 1969, became the first man to step on the moon.

A MOST CHARMING FELLOW

One month later, The Olympic Hotel became host to royalty once again when Prince Philip, Duke of Edinburgh, checked in for his visit to the fair. Flying his own plane from Kamloops, British Columbia, he became the first British royal to set foot in Seattle. Accompanying the dashing prince were a Scotland Yard officer, dressed in tweed and smoking a curved-stem pipe, and the duke's valet, immaculately dressed in black.

Seattleites, especially the ladies, were smitten with the dapper gentleman. The following morning, after the prince fortified himself with a three-bag pot of tea, he took the elevator to the lobby. Elevator operator Pat Farrow told the press, "The elevator was going down but I had the strangest sensation I was going upward."

The prince personified British urbanity. During a chat with the prince, hotel manager Thomas Gildersleve mentioned that he had to go home to change clothes for the dinner to be held that night in the prince's honor. His Royal Highness replied, "You mean the hotel is so full you can't find a room to change?" The prince tossed off comments like this everywhere he went. At the fair, upon seeing rambunctious lads darting in and around the International Fountain, the prince noted, "You always have trouble with small boys. I have one myself." He was referring of course to Prince Charles.

SUBJECTS OF CONVERSATION

Prince Philip enjoyed his day at the fair, and was especially intrigued with the monorail, which he felt might be the answer to mass-transit problems in large cities. Back at the hotel, His Royal Highness attended a reception and dinner in the Spanish Ballroom given by the English-Speaking Union. When asked if Seattle's rainy weather was to his liking, he pointed out that mists and drizzles, "prevent the dreaded dehydration which shrivels the brain, makes sluggish the blood and dims the moist and flashing eye. And, of course, provide an endless subject for conversation."

The next day he went on a tour of the university's fisheries department. Then it was on to the Boeing plant. In one section, an engineer greeted him with, "Welcome to the anthropometric and ergonomic facility, sir!" Prince Philip beamed. "Oh, do say that again," he exclaimed.

His stay in Seattle complete, the Prince boarded his Royal Air Force Heron at Boeing Field. Settling into the pilot's seat, he checked his instruments, then taxied out to the runway. In less time than the tip of a hat and the wink of an eye, he was up into the sky and gone.

Olympic parking garage under construction, 1964.

PARKING SPACE

In the midst of all the progress being celebrated by the World's Fair, Western Hotels management was also looking to the future. In July 1962 plans were announced for a new parking garage to be built across Seneca Street between 4th and 5th avenues. The garage would include a terminal for airport limousines and buses, and would be connected to the hotel via a skybridge. Atop the hotel roof, a helicopter pad was being built to shuttle guests to Bellevue.

This meant the end of the old garage east of the hotel — the former Ice Arena, now almost 50-years-old. The regents who pooh-poohed its construction in 1915 would most likely be amazed that the edifice had lasted so long.

The University of Washington regents of 1962 welcomed the new garage, especially since the hotel was picking up the tab for construction costs. Ground was broken in December under the eye of Eddie Carlson, Thomas Gildersleve, and others connected with the hotel. Also present was Miss Olympic Hotel Garage, who wore a sash and bathing suit for the cameras, in the cold December air.

BUSINESS AS USUAL

After the World's Fair ended, things got back to normal at the hotel. The next big conclave to come to town was the Veterans of Foreign Wars convention, held at the end of August 1963. More than 15,000 veterans attended, and

sessions were split between The Olympic Hotel and the Seattle Center Opera House. One attendee, 88-year-old Ben Lloyd, had fought in the Philippines in 1899, and had attended the founding of the VFW in Pittsburgh in 1914.

The Golden Lion had established itself as one of the premier dining spots in Seattle, providing unique touches unmatched by any other restaurant. Turbaned waiters attended each guest, and it was a privilege to be served by head waiter Orthel Lathan. Guests were serenaded by the Golden Strings of the Lionettes, who positioned themselves about the room, adding a stereophonic sound to their violins.

The 1964 presidential campaign once again brought both party nominees to town and to The Olympic Hotel. Barry Goldwater arrived first, and gave a speech at the Coliseum. More than 14,000 Republicans were there, making it one of the largest campaign rallies in the city up until that time.

Back at the hotel, Goldwater stayed in the Presidential Suite, where he was swarmed in the hallway by well-wishers, many of them teenagers. One boy sported a pin that read, "If I were 21, I'd vote for Barry." The throng included teenaged "Goldwater Girls," who wore blue skirts, white blouses, and white cowboy hats.

President Lyndon B. Johnson arrived at the hotel on September 16, 1964, one week after Goldwater's departure. Johnson pressed the flesh with just about every hand extended to him, and attended a fundraising dinner held in both the Grand and Spanish ballrooms. Back in his suite, the president's meals were quite modest. For breakfast he indulged in a second helping of Crenshaw melon, but for lunch he had just chicken soup, crackers, and decaffeinated coffee.

Olympic Hotel luggage tag.

POLITICAL PARTIES

Modernization continued at the hotel, under the watchful eye of general manager Al E. Schilling Sr., known to many as "Mr. Olympic." More than $1.5 million was spent renovating all the bathrooms and installing air-conditioning in all the rooms. The Olympic was the first major hotel in Seattle to have air-conditioning. The lobby was redecorated, and 5,467 lineal yards of carpeting were laid in the ballrooms, mezzanine, and lobby. And the guest room televisions? New ones were installed with living color.

In 1966, Vice President Hubert Humphrey spoke at a dinner sponsored by the Puget Sound Ocean-ography Study Group. Although his talk was non-partisan, about 60 antiwar picketers marched outside the hotel, protesting the administration's Vietnam policies.

Inside the hotel, everyone in the Spanish Ballroom received identification pins according to their status. Hotel employees wore round gold lapel pins and security personnel wore yellow and gold buttons. Secret Servicemen wore red, blue, and grey emblems, and the press wore white cards with a red slash. Governor Dan Evans wore a Republican elephant tie tack. Democrat party officials were upset because the color chosen for their VIPs was pink.

In 1968, one of the year's largest campaign crowds gathered in University Plaza to see presidential nominee Richard Nixon. More than 5,000 people jammed the street to hear the candidate talk from a speaker's platform set up in front of the entrance. Cheers from the crowd drowned out the antiwar chants of 30 members of the Peace and Freedom Party, who had set up their own public address system across the street.

SMILE WITH THE NILE

The Shriners came back to Seattle in 1969 for the largest convention the city had ever seen. Once again, The Olympic Hotel was chosen as convention headquarters, but the 100,000 fez-wearing funsters that came to town filled hotels from Tumwater to Mount Vernon. Greeting the grand pooh-bahs as they checked into the hotel was a life-sized plush camel wearing a fez. The convention began on July 1 with a standing-room-only opening ceremony in the Grand Ballroom, and lasted until the July 4th weekend.

A huge parade was held on July 1, which rivaled any Seafair parade. More than 8,000 Shriners marched up 4th Avenue to Seattle Center. Led by Grand Marshal Senator Henry M. Jackson — himself a member of the Nile Temple — the parade was filled with horses, a camel, an elephant, miniature cars, clowns (one rode a motorized bathtub with a taxi meter), go-karts, and other small vehicles. When asked why there were so many motorcycles, one Shriner responded, "Some of these guys are too old to walk, but they can ride motorcycles."

At the convention, the Shriner of the Year award went to silent film star Harold Lloyd, for all the charity work he had done for Shriners Hospitals. From

his film days, Lloyd is best remembered as the man hanging off the dial of a giant clock on a building tower in *Safety Last*. Proving that you can't keep a good man down, the 76-year-old comedian had his picture taken on the very top of the Space Needle by *The Seattle Times*. Just outside the workmen's hatch, the Seattle skyline frames Lloyd, who is straddling the guardrail as if hanging on for dear life.

TROUBLE BEGINS TO BREW

As the 1970s began, signs of trouble appeared for The Olympic Hotel. During the 1960s the number of hotel rooms near the airport had increased from 350 to more than 2,000, and that number was growing. This affected all downtown hotels. Between 1969 and 1972, the occupancy rate at The Olympic fell from 75 percent to 59.7 percent. Hotels generally had to have a rate of 70 percent just to break even.

Concerned with its investment, the University of Washington negoti-ated a new lease, which would last only until 1982. The new lease increased Western Hotels' rent from $500,000 to $750,000, but the hotel would not

TOP: *President Lyndon Johnson campaigns in the Grand Ballroom;*
ABOVE: *Protestors outside The Olympic, where Vice President Hubert Humphrey is speaking inside, September 28, 1966.*

have to pay the university a percentage of income unless it met a specified amount.

The regents stressed that no plans were in the works to replace the building, but they were quick to point out that by the time the lease expired the building would be more than 50-years-old. Something needed to be done.

FORESHADOWED PRESIDENTS

On June 3, 1974, The Olympic once again hosted the National Governors Conference, an event that was slightly overshadowed by the news that Seattle had just been awarded a National Football League franchise. President Richard Nixon was invited to the conference, but declined. He was in the darkest days of the Watergate scandal and would resign from office two months later. Nevertheless, two future presidents whose political careers were in ascendancy attended the conference.

A major topic under discussion by the governors was health care. Massachusetts Senator Edward M. Kennedy attended to pitch one of three health-insurance proposals then being discussed by Congress. One of the most vocal opponents to Kennedy's plan was California Governor Ronald Reagan, who stated, "All the talk about a crying health care need in America is a fallacy."

Reagan called for two press conferences while staying at the hotel, leading some to believe that he would soon be running for national office. When questioned about this, Reagan acted surprised and changed the subject. Others thought that Georgia Governor Jimmy Carter might soon be looking at a run in 1976, but Carter claimed he was neutral and was more concerned with helping Democrats in 1974.

WHAT NEXT?

At the end of June, The Olympic Hotel hosted the National Association of the Deaf's annual convention, and 40 hotel employees took sign-language classes in preparation for the event. According to the Association, this was the first of its convention hotels that had ever done such a thing. The Olympic later won an award for these endeavors.

The Marine Room closed in July. The fish tanks were emptied and Olympic General Manager Warren Anderson delivered the exotic fish free of charge to the Central Area Motivation Project, for the children of CAMP's Head Start program. Replacing the Marine Room was The Downstairs, which opened in September, and was later renamed the Yellow Submarine Room. Decorated in hues of red, orange, purple, and silver, the room booked con-

Bandleader Jackie Souders chats with a dancing couple, ca. 1960.

temporary acts of rock and country, and provided discotheque-style music during happy hour from disc jockey John Maynard.

In November, The Olympic turned 50, and many were wondering where its future lay. Although the lease on the hotel didn't expire until 1982, the consensus was that a plan had to be completed by the end of 1975 for restoring it, adding a tower, or tearing it down. Recently the White-Henry-Stuart buildings across the street had been demolished. Was The Olympic next?

SAVE THE OLYMPIC!

Problems with the old hotel were obvious. Many of the rooms were too small, especially those in the 1929 addition to the east wing, which — at the time — had favored traveling salesman. Style was also an issue. Red and gold plush (an Eddie Carlson favorite) was not a desirable look for a grand hotel. Neither was the worn-out model of the Space Needle in the lobby, the chrome, Naugahyde, and plastic décor of the Olympic Bowl, or the stuck windows and peeling wallpaper in the guest rooms.

Everyone had an opinion on what to do with The Olympic Hotel. Architect Minoru Yamasaki, who designed the IBM building east of the hotel as well as New York's World Trade Center, recommended that The Olympic be demolished and replaced with something more "compatible."

On November 15, 1974, a letter signed by 17 prominent citizens — including preservation activist Victor Steinbrueck and Director of the Seattle Department of Community Development and former Allied Arts president (and future mayor) Paul Schell — was delivered to University of Washington regents requesting that The Olympic be remodeled, "into an elegant historic hotel." One week later, the regents called for hotel consultants to make a study on the future of the building.

SITTIN' ON A FENCE

The first task the consultants undertook was a public hearing. Nearly 100 people showed up, almost all of them pleading to save the hotel. Victor Steinbrueck argued that the hotel was a significant landmark, both culturally and historically. James M. Ryan, president of University Properties (later renamed UNICO), called The Olympic, "the single most important traffic generator in the tract."

Many felt that modifications from the 1960s and 1970s, including this walkway over the lobby, were unbefitting to a grand hotel.

By the 1970s, Eddie Carlson revamped much of The Olympic with his favorite colors: red, gold, and dark brown.

Marine Room cocktail compass and matches with Golden Lion swizzle stick.

Two months later, the study recommended a list of 24 alternatives ranging from a park site to a new high-rise hotel to a major remodel. Although the public had been scrambling for an answer, now people needed some time to mull things over. Even Jim Ellis, chairman of the regents' Metropolitan Tract committee, noted that there was no urgency in making a decision. The hotel was aging, but there was still time.

That same month, The Rolling Stones booked rooms in the hotel, and Mick Jagger was asked what it felt like to grow old. Unaware of the irony, he responded, "What I was doing when I was 18 I'm doing now. I mean the room I had at the Olympic Hotel in Seattle is the same room I would have had in 1964. I mean it wasn't any grander; it was the same room. And I'm doing the same things, slightly different of course . . . don't know if it's good or bad, because I can't evaluate it . . . I don't feel responsibilities other people feel. I don't worry about the future."

HEAVY READING

The Olympic welcomed another presidential visitor in 1975. This time it was Gerald Ford, in town for a "Presidential Town Hall Meeting" with six of his cabinet members. Before arriving at the hotel for a luncheon with GOP contributors, a bomb threat was called in. The Secret Service made a sweep of the hotel, found nothing, and the lunch went on as planned.

In September 1975, the university's study team released their preliminary report — a document that weighed four pounds. The consultants felt that the hotel had substantial economic value despite its drawbacks, but the proposed solutions were many. The most attractive plan, in their opinion, was to clean up the exterior, remodel the interior, and to knock out walls, converting 764 small rooms into 450 larger rooms.

The team's other proposals included adding two floors to the existing structure, building a 260-room tower atop the southwest corner, and demolishing the hotel and replacing it with a 1,000-room tower. More public discussion ensued.

THE STARS COME OUT

Meanwhile, television viewers across America got to see the Spanish Ballroom in all its glory in a scene filmed for the TV movie *Eleanor and Franklin*. The ballroom was chosen for the Roosevelt biopic because The Olympic was one of the few hotels in America that had an architectural style that matched the era of the 1920s. Yet this was not The Olympic's movie debut. The lobby and exterior had a cameo in the 1973 theatrical film, *Harry in Your Pocket*.

In the spring of 1976, the hotel once again hosted royalty, when King Carl XVI Gustaf of Sweden came to town during his 26-day tour of the states. Soon after he checked in, he and his party had dinner at Ivar's Captain Table, owned by restaurateur Ivar Haglund, who was of Swedish descent. For a short time in the 1930s, Ivar had actually worked in the kitchens of The Olympic Hotel before going on to achieve local fame with his "Acres of Clams." The next night the King attended a banquet held in his honor at The Olympic sponsored by the Seattle Swedish Community Bicentennial Committee.

One of the most unlikely musical acts in Olympic history played at the hotel in 1977 — The Ramones, one of the first, if not the first punk rock bands in the country. The group was on their first West Coast tour, and whoever booked them at The Olympic most likely knew little about them, because they played a Sunday night show in the Georgian Room. The band didn't know many songs yet, and after taking a break following a 20-minute first set, they came back to play the same songs all over again.

AW, SHUCKS!

By 1977, it was no secret that Western Hotels was dissatisfied with running The Olympic, although the managers claimed that they wished to stay on past 1982, especially since their corporate offices were located in the hotel's penthouse.

In March, Western announced plans to build a 40-story office-hotel tower across Seneca and connected to the original building, which would be refurbished. A sigh of relief went out from those wishing to see the old hotel saved, but their elation was short-lived. In June, Western gave up the tower plan. Once again, the future was in limbo.

While top managers ironed out the problems, the hotel staff continued their daily routine. In June 1978, general manager Frank Finneran announced the opening of Shuckers, a clam and oyster bar on the corner of 4th Avenue and Seneca Street. Finneran and his staff came up with the restaurant idea after five years of marginal success for the Piccadilly Corner, an English pub in the same location. Shuckers was designed like a bakeshop. Passersby could peer through the window and see oysters being shucked and grilled. The restaurant and bar proved successful and is still operating today.

JUMPING THE GUN

In the spring of 1978, Elliott Bay Associates and the Pacific Seaboard Group made an offer to take over and renovate the hotel in conjunction with Inter-Continental Hotels, a subsidiary of Pan-American Airways. Local investors, including Paul Schell and Dick Clotfelter, presented a $20 million plan that would refurbish all public spaces and replace the Grand Ballroom with retail space and a glass atrium.

The regents refused to consider the plan, stating it was too early and that proposals would not be accepted until November. Over the summer, an environmental impact statement was released which stated that replacing the hotel would be financially advantageous for the university. When the public got wind of this, another cry went up to save The Olympic Hotel.

At the end of the year, the regents called for proposals. The local investors resubmitted their plan, and The Hyatt Corp. of Chicago, Sheffield Hotels of Anchorage, and Four Seasons of Toronto submitted letters of interest. Missing was Western Hotels, which had asked to be released from its lease, to which the regents agreed.

The regents also listened to the concerns of the public, especially after the outcry that resulted when the White-Henry-Stuart buildings were torn down to make way for Rainier Square. The public was not willing to let go of its "Grand Dame." A six-month extension was placed on delivery of the proposals, and the regents stipulated that submittals must not include demolition of The Olympic. The old hotel was saved.

DAWN OF A NEW ERA

On June 19, 1979, the university received proposals from three firms: The Hyatt, the Four Seasons, and Inter-Continental. All of the plans retained most of the original public spaces, and included no changes to the exterior shell of the hotel. The Hyatt and Four Seasons plans called for closing the hotel during reconstruction for up to 18 months.

Interviews were held with each prospective operator on July 9 and 10. On July 14, the regents, in a unanimous decision, chose Four Seasons. The hotel chain, in a joint venture with JMB Realty of Chicago, would pay the university $450,000 a year for two years, followed by a base rent of $1.26 million a year afterwards. More would be paid after room rents and other income increased. Dick Clotfelter and Paul Schell balked at the decision, noting that one of the university consultants had previously worked with the Four Seasons. The regents found no conflict of interest and stood by their choice.

One month after the decision, The Olympic Hotel was officially placed on the National Register of Historic Places. City conservator J. M. Neil noted that the proposal chosen by the regents appeared to be compatible with national register standards. Preparations soon began for the closure of

Grand Staircase as seen from the Assembly Lounge, ca. 1980.

Chapter 4

THE LEGACY RENEWED

TOP: *University Street entrance, ca. 1980;* ABOVE: *Architectural drawing of the proposed University Street entrance, 1980.*

*T*he Four Seasons plan detailed many upcoming changes to the hotel. The most noticeable from the street would be the demolition of the Grand Ballroom and construction of a new entrance on University Street. Seattle architects NBBJ (Naramore, Bain, Brady, and Johanson), in charge of design, also called for a health club and swimming pool to be placed above the lobby facing Seneca Street.

Inside the hotel, retail space would take the place of the Golden Lion and Olympic Grill, and the Georgian Room would reclaim its role as the hotel's main dining room. All the public spaces would be returned to 1920s elegance. Walls would be torn out in all 756 guest rooms, resulting in a new total of 450 large rooms, including 201 deluxe rooms, 10 suites, and two VIP apartment suites. In the deluxe rooms, bedrooms would be separated from seating areas by floor-to-ceiling French doors.

Arrangements were made with Western Hotels to transfer the lease early. A new 60-year lease was written up for Four Seasons. Remodeling was slated to begin in October 1980, giving the hotel enough time to accommodate conventions that had booked in advance. Groups booked after that date were rescheduled or relocated to other hotels.

LAST CALL

On September 21, 1980, the last political fundraiser before the remodel was held for Senator Warren Magnuson, who had been a member of Congress since 1936. This year, "Maggie" was in a heated Senate race with Slade Gorton, which Magnuson eventually lost. When The Olympic closed down, he also lost his room, which he had claimed as his Washington state voter's residence since 1934.

Over the years, various people had permanent residence status in the hotel. Ten days before closure, one couple moved out who had lived in the same suite since 1933. From 1930 to 1936, Clarence Blethen, publisher of *The Seattle Times,* lived in the penthouse apartment. When Teamster boss Dave Beck was released from prison after serving time for grand larceny, he moved into the hotel under the name Mr. Sweet. Probably the most well-known resident was boxing promoter "Deacon" Jack Hurley.

The closing of the hotel meant that the 711 employees were out of a job. Almost 600 of them were members of the Hotel, Motel, Restaurant Employees and Bartenders' Union. Each received a severance pay of $100 plus $20 for each year of service. Some employees went to look for other work; others retired. Seventy-year-old Earl Woodson, who had shined shoes in the barbershop for 30 years, put away his saddle soap. Tubby Clark played his last sweet song in the Golden Lion. Many in the audience cried.

The final event held in the hotel before it shut down was the "Last Grand Affair," a benefit party for Children's Orthopedic Hospital. Socialite and clothing designer Gloria Vanderbilt was a special guest, and 700 of Seattle's finest attended to raise money and reminisce about past events at The Olympic. The highlight of the evening was a fashion gala presented by the Bon Marché in which models dressed and performed dances of each decade from the 1920s on. At the end of the fundraiser, those who had paid double for tickets stayed on for a separate party to bid the hotel bon voyage, until they met again.

COMMUNITY CONCERNS

The remodel of The Olympic Hotel presented many challenges, not the least of which was to allay community concerns over many issues. To handle public relations, Four Seasons management hired C. David Hughbanks, who for years had been involved with many of the city's civic events, including Seafair.

His first order of business was assuring the citizenry that although the total number of rooms in the hotel would diminish, larger

Original guest-room keys were framed and presented to select VIPs, 1980.

rooms would attract more guests. Local preservationists were told that the Canadian and Chicago developers would strive to maintain the historic significance of one of Seattle's most well-loved buildings. Diners bemoaned the loss of the hotel's signature hard rolls, until they were informed that the kitchen had stopped baking them more than a decade ago, and had been buying them wholesale ever since.

Almost everyone, it seemed, had questions. During the remodel, what will happen to the hotel retailers? Why get rid of the skybridges? How will pedestrians be able navigate the sidewalks during construction? Are you really tearing down the Grand Ballroom? Where will we hold our Christmas balls, charity events, weddings, and Bar Mitzvahs? All these queries and more were answered in an intense public relations campaign that lasted for two years, if not longer.

SALE OF THE CENTURY

Even before The Olympic closed for remodeling, the front desk was inundated with calls from people who wanted to buy old room keys. Charity groups were given the keys for fundraising purposes, but those who wanted to own part of the hotel's past had plenty of opportunity. On October 16, possibly the largest rummage sale in Seattle history opened for business, as the hotel sold off just about everything — including the kitchen sink.

The public sale lasted for 60 days, but on the first day the line stretched around the block as thousands arrived with the hopes of buying a piece of history, or maybe just getting a bargain. Only 150 people were let into the hotel at a time. Awaiting them were 10,000 pieces of dinnerware and silverware, 11,000 twin-size bed sheets, 5,000 double-bed sheets, and numerous vacuum cleaners, ashtrays, beds, dressers, drapes, and sinks, as well as 750 color TVs equipped with AM/FM radios.

Big-ticket items included an upright piano, a 30-foot cocktail bar, a massive walnut board-of-directors' table, 10,000 feet of oak flooring from the Grand Ballroom, and the ballroom's chandeliers. Even the doors to the guest rooms were up for grabs. Within weeks, the building was picked clean, except for the original 1920s chandeliers in the lobby.

BUILT TO LAST

Demolition and construction began soon after. First to go was the Grand Ballroom. The guest rooms were stripped down to structural essentials, and some of the walls between them were broken out to create larger rooms. Sandblasting was performed on the exterior, returning the sandstone from dingy gray back to a mellow tan. More than 10,000 cubic yards of debris was hauled away, including the skybridge between the hotel and the garage.

Once the contractors were able to examine the superstructure, they were pleasantly surprised by its condition. There were no large cracks anywhere, and even more remarkably, the building was no more than one-eighth inch out of plumb. These findings allowed work to go forward smoothly, although later the university and Four Seasons got into a squabble over who should pay for the seismic retrofit. The regents shook $5.6 million out of their pockets.

In the Georgian Room, blackout paint from World War II was finally chipped off the windows. In the Spanish Ballroom, the oak paneling was removed to install seismic bracing. The wood — which had been stained dark in the 1950s — was stripped, bleached, refinished to its original shade, and replaced. The same was done to all the wood in all the public rooms. Damaged wood was replaced with oak shipped from England, and cutting blades were located that matched the same flitch.

MYSTERIOUS FINDS

During the remodel the contactors found some interesting surprises. Plumbers were intrigued by the original cold water lines, which were larger at the top of the building than they were at the bottom. This was because the 1924 system was designed to be gravity fed from a reservoir on the roof.

Deep in the basement, workers found an odd machine that had

Architectural drawing of the proposed restoration of the Lobby, 1980.

been there since the beginning. It was an antique sock press that could steampress 12 pairs of hosiery all at once. Considered high-tech in the 1920s, it was now one of the few of its kind in existence.

Workers found memos, correspondence, and other paperwork that once belonged to Albert S. Kerry, The Olympic Hotel's first president. An urn was found inside the walls of Shuckers that contained the ashes of a couple who had met at The Olympic during World War II and wished to become part of the building. But the most mysterious discovery was a wall safe in the manager's office that had been hidden behind a painting for years. It took a locksmith with a drill to open it up. What was inside? Nothing.

REOPENING DAY

The Four Seasons Olympic Hotel opened for business on Sunday, May 23, 1982. The first registered guests were Albert Kerry — son of Albert Kerry Sr. — and his wife Audrey, who had attended the grand opening in 1924. This time, Mr. Kerry attempted to sign in as Albert Kerry and wife, but Audrey stopped him. "It's a new world," she said. "I'm signing for myself."

At first, only 50 rooms were available. Additional guest rooms became available over the next few months until the hotel became fully operational in July. Throughout the day, general manager Charles Ferraro greeted visitors while coordinating his staff to make sure that all was running smoothly. Because the hotel opened in sections, the term "soft opening" was born in Seattle.

Guests entering the lobby from the Seneca Street entrance looked up to see 13 six-foot chandeliers — the same ones that were installed in 1924, completely restored to their former brilliance. Those entering on the University Street side saw a brand new lobby that connected to the original one by escalators. The Seneca Lobby, as well as the Spanish Ballroom, looked as new as when the hotel opened in 1924.

Exploring the main area, many made their way to the Garden Court Lounge, a skylit fern- and ficus-filled room that had replaced the Grand Ballroom. Others looked in on the pool and spa that overlooked Seneca Street from the second floor terrace. On the mezzanine, new conference rooms were available for business professionals. Half a level down, larger meetings could be held in the distinctive Metropole Room, once the Olympic Bowl, which had replaced the Italian Ballroom.

The entire restoration cost more than $62.5 million, more than 10 times the cost of the original hotel, and it showed. Rave reviews appeared in newspapers statewide, and then across the nation. But although response to the new hotel was positive, the opening was not without controversy.

LABOR PAINS

During the 18-month reconstruction period, the hotel union contract had lapsed and become null. In the interim, more than 13,000 people applied for

The Lobby during restoration, 1981.

The Georgian Room during restoration, 1981.

600 positions. When the Four Seasons reopened the hotel, it did so without union contracts. A coalition of 21 unions representing restaurant, hotel, and service personnel, called WEST, pushed to organize the new workers.

General manager Charles Ferraro refused to allow union organizers into the premises to talk with employees, stating that it was the opinion of the Four Seasons company that there was no advantage for the employees to seek outside representation. The unions began a boycott and soon brought out picket signs. WEST ran newspaper and television ads accusing Four Seasons of breaking faith with Seattle's tradition of labor representation and the hotel's own community roots. One ad in the *Wall Street Journal* "advised" travelers to avoid The Four Seasons Olympic until the dispute was resolved.

Union leaders won support from Mayor Charles Royer and Congressmen Mike Lowry, Norm Dicks, Don Bonker, and Al Swift. U.S. Senator Henry M. Jackson attempted to broker a compromise, but Mario Vacarino, powerful president of Hotel Employees and Restaurant Employees Union Local 8, rebuffed his efforts. A year later, for as yet unknown reasons, Vacarino was brutally murdered in his bathtub.

Formal charges were brought against The Four Seasons Olympic claiming that the hotel had improperly interrogated applicants about their personal feelings toward unions. Labor leaders also accused Four Seasons management of age and sex discrimination in new hiring. The National Labor Relations Board later rejected both charges, and the active

Architectural drawing of the proposed restoration of the Georgian Room, 1980.

boycott ultimately faded away. The Four Seasons remained on union "unfair lists," however, putting it off-limits for most public officials and candidates, especially Democrats. Thus, The Olympic's star at the center of Seattle's political universe dimmed. But it continued to be "The Hotel" to Seattle's social elite, as well as to upscale business guests and vacationers.

NOTEWORTHY EVENT

On July 10, 1982, all the work on the hotel was now complete and The Four Seasons Olympic held its grand opening gala. Valet parking — unheard of at the time for a Seattle hotel — was provided for guests. A fundraiser was held in the Spanish Ballroom for the Seattle Symphony, but outside the building more than 400 union members protested the hotel's non-union status. The picket line was informational, and attendees to the fundraiser were told that The Four Seasons Olympic was not a struck hotel.

Only six people declined to cross the picket line while 250 people attended the event. The Seattle Symphony was more than $1 million in debt, and, at $250 per ticket, the guest list read like a who's who of Seattle's arts patrons. Governor Dan Evans was in attendance, as was Jeanette Rockefeller, who had just moved back to Seattle. Mrs. Rockefeller was the widow of Arkansas Governor Winthrop Rockefeller, and the daughter of the hotel's previous owner, William Edris.

Symphony supporters dined on lobster and veal. Hundreds of rose bouquets were spread throughout the hotel. The highlight for the evening was a performance by jazz great Oscar Peterson, a surprise gift to the party from the Four Seasons management. Peterson flew in from the East Coast and flew back the same night on the hotel's tab.

STORES AND MORE

In the fall of 1982, it was announced that there would be 14 new street-level retail shops. Many of them opened before Christmas. Abercrombie & Fitch was the keystone shop, and filled much of the space once occupied by the Golden Lion. Other businesses included Laura Ashley, Ltd. and Gene Juarez hair salon.

In December 1984, new historical plaques went up at the hotel, while others were moved. The UW regents installed a plaque honoring Daniel Bagley and Arthur Denny, and three plaques now graced a wall next to the University Street entrance: an Albert S. Kerry plaque, a marker installed by the Daughters of the Pioneers in 1924 noting the first location of the university, and a plaque from the U.S. Department of the Interior designating the property on the National Register of Historic Places.

In 1985, the skybridge over 4th Avenue came down. Besides being an eyesore, the structure got very little use. An informal survey done by the *Seattle Post-Intelligencer* found that during lunchtime, only 26 people crossed it over a 100-minute period.

Onward and Upward

The Four Seasons Olympic continued to have cameo roles in major motion pictures. A murder in the 1987 movie *Black Widow* was filmed in the Olympic Suite and in 1994's *Disclosure,* Michael Douglas sneaks into the Cascade Suite. In 1989, the lobby of the hotel was disguised as an ornate piano bar in *The Fabulous Baker Boys,* which filmed other scenes in other parts of the hotel. Even the Olympic Garage made it to the silver screen for a scene in 1987's *House of Games.*

Under Four Seasons management, The Olympic upheld its tradition of holding some of the city's more newsworthy events. In the 1980s, a convention of carnival operators held a dinner in which the Baked Alaska was brought in on the backs of baby elephants. In 1990, the Spanish Ballroom was transformed into ancient Egypt for an American Cancer Society masked ball fundraiser. And in 1999, delegates to the World Trade Organization dined and held meetings in The Olympic while rioters and police clashed throughout downtown Seattle. One week later, at the hotel's 75th birthday party, Seattle Mayor Paul Schell told guests that he would not seek a second term. (He eventually did run in 2001, but lost in the primary.)

Famous visitors came and went. In 1993, eight suites were redecorated for the Sultan of Brunei — the world's richest man. In 1996, civil rights activist Rosa Parks was a guest, as was Israeli Prime Minister Benjamin Netanyahu and Labor Party leader Shimon Peres, followed a few months later by Bill Gates, who held a technology summit to which leaders of the top 100 U.S. corporations were invited. Vice President Al Gore and Washington Governor Gary Locke were featured speakers. In 1997, the entire cast of television's *Frasier* rented rooms while in town to film their 100th episode. That same year Donald Trump was a guest, and in 2002, Steven Spielberg and Tom Cruise took up residence while in town to promote their film *Minority Report.* In 2004, the King and Queen of Spain stayed at The Olympic during their visit to Seattle.

A New Legacy

Soon after the hotel reopened in 1982, it garnered a Five Diamond rating from the American Automobile Association. In 1996, it received a Five Star award by the Mobil Travel Guide — the first such honor in the state — and in 1997, The Olympic was awarded Five-Flag status by Frommer's.

In the late 1990s, JMB Realty — majority owner of the hotel lease — began scouting for prospective buyers for the hotel. At the time, Seattle was in a boom economy, thanks in part to the Internet industry, and the time was right to sell. The dot-com bubble burst soon after the turn of the century, but The Olympic Hotel — steeped in tradition as one of downtown Seattle's most distinctive properties — remained a valuable prize for the right owner.

In 2003, JMB Realty gave Legacy Hotels Real Estate Investment Trust the rare opportunity to acquire the lease and Fairmont Hotels & Resorts to manage the hotel. Fairmont Hotels & Resorts had overseen iconic heritage properties for more than 100 years and was considered to be the ideal management company to protect and steward the legacy of Seattle's landmark Olympic Hotel. The purchase price was $105 million.

Enjoy Your Stay

Just as happened when the Four Seasons took over the hotel in the 1980s, some people in the local business community raised concerns that the hotel was not sold to a Seattle-based firm. But Fairmont was no stranger to the region, as evidenced by their management of the historic Empress Hotel in Victoria, B.C., the Fairmont Hotel Vancouver, and the Fairmont in San Francisco, where they had recently spent $85 million in renovations.

On August 1, 2003, The Four Seasons Olympic became The Fairmont Olympic. The Fairmont flag was proudly placed atop the roof, and Dennis Clark — who had managed Boston's historic Copley Plaza since 1998 — took over as general manager. Almost immediately, plans were in the works for future renovations to The Olympic that would embrace the twenty-first century while respecting the hotel's past.

Our story does not end here, nor is it fully told. The Olympic holds many tales: Some are known, others are not, and many have yet to occur. The ongoing history of The Olympic Hotel is practically a history of Seattle itself. If you've made it this far, you might be interested to learn more.

If so . . . be our guest.

Ornate woodwork appears throughout the hotel, 2004.

The Main Lobby is a superb setting in which to meet with friends or enjoy some quiet time with a book or a laptop computer.

The Garden remains one of the most unique places in Seattle to host a private function.

The Petite Georgian accommodates private dinners off the main dining room.

Shuckers is one of Seattle's original oyster bars, serving fresh and flavorful Northwest seafood and local artisan microbrews in a pub-style setting.

The Georgian, the hotel's award-winning main restaurant, features Northwest cuisine in elegant surroundings.

A modern fitness club and swimming pool now stand above the original Seneca Street entrance.

The Cascade Suite is the signature suite at The Fairmont Olympic Hotel and can accommodate a reception of up to 20 guests. The dining room can accommodate up to 12 guests.

All rooms at The Fairmont Olympic Hotel feature elegant decor with many amenities.

The Spanish Ballroom, whose regal chandeliers have sparkled over the city's most important occasions for more than two generations, sets the hotel's exemplary standards for meetings and events. The historic Ballroom features a spacious foyer and soaring 20-foot ceilings.

The Grand Staircase rises from the 4th Avenue entrance to the Main Lobby, and then higher to the Spanish Foyer and the mezzanine, which features lavishly appointed meeting rooms.

Index

Photo Credits

p. 8.

Territorial University. Courtesy University of Washington Libraries Special Collections.

p. 9.

Seattle waterfront. Courtesy University of Washington Libraries Special Collections.

p. 10.

Students and faculty on university steps. Courtesy University of Washington Libraries Special Collections.

Territorial building columns. Courtesy University of Washington Libraries Special Collections.

p. 11.

Architectural rendering of the White Building and Henry Building. Courtesy University of Washington Libraries Special Collections.

Metropolitan Theatre. Courtesy University of Washington Libraries Special Collections.

p. 12.

Ice Arena. Courtesy University of Washington Libraries Special Collections.

p. 14.

Olympic Hotel. Photo by Asahel Curtis. Courtesy Museum of History and Industry.

p. 15.

Community Hotel Corporation correspondence and note of appreciation. Courtesy The Fairmont Olympic Hotel.

p. 16.

Gold Rush ship. Photo by Edward S. Curtis. Courtesy Museum of History and Industry.

The Olympic Hotel under construction. Courtesy Museum of History and Industry.

p. 17.

Seneca Street entrance. Courtesy Paul Dorpat.

p. 18.

Marine Room and guest room. Courtesy of Museum of History and Industry.

Marine Room ashtray. Courtesy The Fairmont Olympic Hotel.

p. 19.

Assembly Lounge, Lobby, and Spanish Ballroom. Courtesy Museum of History and Industry.

Opening night menu. Courtesy University of Washington Libraries Special Collections.

p. 20.

Assembly Lounge with columns. Courtesy Paul Dorpat.

p. 21.

Curb service. Courtesy Paul Dorpat.

Ad for Eddie Harkness. Courtesy Museum of History and Industry.

p. 22.

Knights Templar arch. Courtesy Paul Dorpat.

Landes and Lindbergh. Courtesy University of Washington Special Collections.

p. 23.

Olympic Hotel brochure. Courtesy The Fairmont Olympic Hotel.

p. 25.

Franklin D. Roosevelt. Courtesy Museum of History and Industry.

p. 26.

J. Edgar Hoover. Courtesy Museum of History and Industry.

Herbert Hoover. Courtesy Museum of History and Industry.

p. 27.

Original artwork. Courtesy Museum of History and Industry.

Personality Parade (Olympic Magazine). Courtesy The Fairmont Olympic Hotel.

Ad for Grill. Courtesy The Fairmont Olympic Hotel.

p. 28.

Victory Square. Courtesy Museum of History and Industry.

p. 29.

Lana Turner. Courtesy Museum of History and Industry.

p. 30.

Ice skaters. Courtesy Museum of History and Industry.

Georgian Room menu. Courtesy The Fairmont Olympic Hotel.

p. 31.

General Douglas MacArthur. Courtesy Museum of History and Industry.

Emperor Haile Selassie. Courtesy Museum of History and Industry.

Metropolitan Theatre demolition. Courtesy Museum of History and Industry.

p. 32.

Baking rolls. Courtesy Museum of History and Industry.

Dining in Georgian Room. Courtesy Museum of History and Industry.

p. 33.

Grand opening, University Street entrance. Courtesy Museum of History and Industry.

Jean Beall mural. Courtesy Museum of History and Industry.

p. 34.

Norman Lavin. Courtesy Museum of History and Industry.

Magnuson and Truman. Courtesy Museum of History and Industry.

Prince Akihito and Princess Michiko. Courtesy Museum of History and Industry.

p. 35.

Eddie Carlson et al. Courtesy Museum of History and Industry.

Marine Room. Courtesy Museum of History and Industry.

p. 36.

Magnuson and JFK. Courtesy Museum of History and Industry.

Governor Nelson Rockefeller. Courtesy Museum of History and Industry.

Barry Goldwater. Courtesy Museum of History and Industry.

John Glenn. Courtesy Museum of History and Industry.

p. 37.

Olympic parking garage. Courtesy Museum of History and Industry.

Luggage tag. Courtesy The Fairmont Olympic Hotel.

p. 38.

President Lyndon Johnson. Courtesy Museum of History and Industry.

Protestors. Courtesy Museum of History and Industry.

p. 39.

Bandleader Jackie Souders. Courtesy Museum of History and Industry,

p. 40.

Lobby modifications. Courtesy The Fairmont Olympic Hotel.

p. 41.

Decor of the 1970s. Courtesy The Fairmont Olympic Hotel.

Cocktail compass. Courtesy Museum of History and Industry.

Matchbook and swizzle stick. Courtesy The Fairmont Olympic Hotel.

p. 43.

Grand staircase. Courtesy The Fairmont Olympic Hotel.

p. 44.

University Street entrance. Photo by Mary Nichols. Courtesy The Fairmont Olympic Hotel.

Architectural drawing. Courtesy The Fairmont Olympic Hotel.

p. 45.

Guest-room keys. Courtesy The Fairmont Olympic Hotel.

p. 46.

Architectural drawing. Courtesy The Fairmont Olympic Hotel.

p. 47.

Lobby during restoration. Courtesy The Fairmont Olympic Hotel.

p. 48.

Georgian Room during restoration. Courtesy The Fairmont Olympic Hotel.

p. 49.

Architectural drawing. Courtesy The Fairmont Olympic Hotel.

p. 51.

Woodwork. Photo by Mary Nichols. Courtesy The Fairmont Olympic Hotel.

p. 52.

Main Lobby. Photo by Robb Gordon. Courtesy The Fairmont Olympic Hotel.

p. 53.

The Garden. Photo by Kim Zumwalt. Courtesy The Fairmont Olympic Hotel.

Shuckers. Courtesy The Fairmont Olympic Hotel.

Petite Georgian Room. Photo by Mary Nichols. Courtesy The Fairmont Olympic Hotel.

p. 54.

Georgian Room. Photo by Mary Nichols. Courtesy The Fairmont Olympic Hotel.

p. 55.

Fitness Club. Photo by Mary Nichols. Courtesy The Fairmont Olympic Hotel.

Cascade Suite and luxury suite. Photo by Mary Nichols. Courtesy The Fairmont Olympic Hotel.

p. 56.

Spanish Ballroom. Photo by Mary Nichols. Courtesy The Fairmont Olympic Hotel.

p. 57.

Grand staircase. Photo by Robb Gordon. Courtesy The Fairmont Olympic Hotel